P9-DVN-515

THE NEW
FINE POINTS OF
FURNITURE
EARLY AMERICAN

THE NEW
FINE POINTS OF
FURNITURE
EARLY AMERICAN

GOOD • BETTER • BEST
SUPERIOR • MASTERPIECE

BETTER   MASTERPIECE   SUPERIOR

BY ALBERT SACK

CROWN PUBLISHERS, INC.   NEW YORK

Copyright © 1993 by Albert Sack

All rights reserved. No part of this book may be reproduced or transmitted in
any form or by any means, electronic or mechanical, including photocopying,
recording, or by any information storage and retrieval system, without
permission in writing from the publisher.

Published by Crown Publishers, Inc., 201 East 50th Street, New York,
New York 10022. Member of the Crown Publishing Group.

Random House, Inc. New York, Toronto, London, Sydney, Auckland.

CROWN is a trademark of Crown Publishers, Inc.

Manufactured in Japan

Book design by June Bennett-Tantillo

Library of Congress Cataloging-in-Publication Data
Albert Sack.
The new fine points of furniture :
Early American, good, better, best, superior,
masterpiece / by Albert Sack. — 1st ed.
p. cm
Includes bibliographical references and index.
1. Furniture, Early American. I. Title.
NK2046.S292 1993 749.214—dc20
93-7127 CIP

ISBN 0-517-58820-X

10 9 8 7 6 5 4 3 2 1

First Edition

To my devoted wife, Shirley,
who inspired me to undertake this project
and who would not let me
give up when the obstacles
seemed overwhelming

CONTENTS

ACKNOWLEDGMENTS

The story of the completion of this book could not be told without the record of rescues and rescuers. The contract was signed with Crown Publishers fully four years ago and their patience and unwavering support through the many lapses of deadlines have been inspirational.

I soon came to realize that there was far more to writing a book such as this than merely selecting and gathering the comparisons and writing the captions. The prodigious effort of editing the comparisons and content, forming liaisons and corresponding with museums and individuals, left me overwhelmed. Deanne Levison, who had recently joined our firm as consultant, stepped into the breach. With her boundless energy and unmatched professional competence, she took over the structuring of the material. She devoted hundreds of hours to contacting museums and individuals for photographs and credits. She helped me structure the order of the material and, most of all, reviewed the comparisons. Our constant discussions and critiques helped us to improve or revise the comparisons. I wanted to recognize her input on the title page, but she modestly declined. Nevertheless, without her input, efforts, and talent, this book would hardly have been possible.

More recently, our exceptional young assistant, Alicia Altman Southwell, has been continuing the enormous task of collating the material, continuing to contact museums and individuals, and attending to the infinite details required to finish the manuscript. Most important, she has continued to make me toe the mark when my aversion to detail has inhibited the progress.

From the beginning, Mary Dobbin, secretary at Israel Sack, Inc., has devotedly typed all the captions and manuscript of this book, often retyping the material when revisions were made. Her tireless efforts, her patience with my constant changes, and her encouragement in the face of the many setbacks spurred me to continue.

A majority of the photographs contained in this book have been obtained from the extensive files of Israel Sack, Inc., including many of the illustrations of pieces formerly owned by the company and now credited to their present owners. James Conzo, as the photographer for Israel Sack, Inc., has been responsible for many of the photographs reproduced in this book, particularly the excellent color illustrations. He has also performed some miraculous reproductions of pages from books and catalogues when photographs were not available.

A special thanks goes to Sotheby's and Christie's auction houses for opening their files to me. The vast amount and range of objects of all grades that have passed through their hands have enabled me to make some astonishing comparisons of forms similar in concept but varying in quality. The most difficult task in a book such as this is to find illustrations of items to complete the comparisons being made. The fact that I drew on their material mostly to avail myself of items for the GOOD and BETTER categories is in no way meant to demean the contribution of those galleries which have, simultaneously, handled innumerable great objects and masterpieces. Their staffs, therefore, demonstrated their dedication to scholarship and their faith that their contribution would serve that goal. My particular thanks to Bill Stahl and Monica Sands.

A major discovery which provided the source of many illustrations was the Photographic Archives of the National Gallery of Art. Jerry Mallick of that gallery was especially helpful in supplying the photographs I selected from their files. The Photographic Archives is an incredible and little-known resource and should be drawn on more extensively by scholars.

My brother Robert Sack helped me prepare some of the material, photographs, and slides. He and my brother Harold have been most generous in allowing me to use so much material from our files.

In addition to these acknowledgments, I owe a great deal to the many private collectors who have helped in the writing of this book in numerous ways. Among these collectors are: Mr. and Mrs. Robert Aller; Mr. and Mrs. Isaac Arnold; Mr. and Mrs. John S. Barker; Mr. and Mrs. Robert M. Bass; Mr. and Mrs. Marvin Baten; Mr. and Mrs. Edward Berner; Diane and Norman Bernstein; Mr. and Mrs. Peter M. Brant; Mr. and Mrs. Thomas G. Cousins; Mr. and Mrs. William O. de Witt, Jr.; Mr. William K. du Pont; Mr. William S. Farish, III; Mr. and Mrs. William Freehling; Dr. and Mrs. John C. Garrett; Dr. and Mrs. Mark Gold; Dr. Robert Halper; Mr. and Mrs. G. Fenimore Johnson; Mr. and Mrs. Edward A. Kilroy, Jr.; Mr. and Mrs. William S. Kilroy; Mr. and Mrs. Ronald Lauder; Mr. and Mrs. Israel Liverant; Mrs. Screven Lorillard; Mr. A. Lotterman; Peter and Carolyn Lynch; Mary Ann Burgess McCrea; Mr. and Mrs. James R. McNab, Jr.; Mr. and Mrs. Robert L. McNeil, Jr.; Dr. and Mrs. Matthew Newman; Mr. and Mrs. Eddy G. Nicholson; Mr. and Mrs. E. J. Nusrala; Mr. and Mrs. Laird Park, Jr.; Mr. Arthur Robson, Jr.; Mr. and Mrs. Irvin Schorsch, Jr.; Mrs. E. Newbold Smith; Martha and Lane Stokes; Roberta T. and Samuel H. Vickers; and Mr. and Mrs. E. Martin Wunsch.

FOREWORD

T he publication in 1950 of the book *Fine Points of Furniture: Early American* was to have a far greater impact on the field of American decorative arts than the author ever envisioned. Albert Sack joined his brother Harold and their father, the renowned and respected Israel Sack, in business in 1934. In addition to judging American furniture in regard to authenticity, they evaluated the form, line, and proportion, craftsmanship, and, ultimately, the degree of successful expression of artistic merit of any given piece. Albert's deep appreciation for the achievements of early American furniture craftsmen and his developed eye for quality led him to put some of his observations in print. Most often referred to over the years as "Good, Better, and Best," this book was the first to compare specific forms of American furniture from a standpoint of aesthetic attainment. The approach of pictorially showing similar pieces of a given form and describing why one represented a more successful presentation than another resulted in an invaluable aid in developing the eye of the beginner and in honing that of the more experienced collector or scholar. No one had ever organized and published such an analysis, and the ease with which the author led the reader to visually rate each piece was clearly evidenced by the continuous demand for the book. Attesting both to the gap it filled in printed material focusing on American decorative arts and to its universal acceptance as a cornerstone for any library on the subject is the fact that it was reprinted over twenty-five times in the past forty years.

As was explained in the essay "Collecting Antiques" in the earlier book, furniture of varying degrees of both sophistication and level of mastery was made throughout the colonies. Even outside urban high-style centers, certain cabinetmakers plied their talents to create exceptional expressions of development. Seldom are these pieces signed or labeled, and the final analysis must, therefore, generally be made by judgment of the product itself. This was the premise upon which such an approach as "Good, Better, and Best" was conceived.

Looking at furniture is perhaps no different than looking at any other art form. Although there can be an initial emotional or mental reaction to anything one sees, a developed, trained eye adds immeasurably not only to understanding the object but also to the appreciation of, and finally the conscious or unconscious ranking of, the object within its given category.

The New Fine Points of Furniture: Early American is far more than a mere revision of the previous book. The comparisons are more comprehensive, the text is more in-depth, and two new categories have been added. The author's critical eye and encompassing analytical ability again explain the basic concepts of evaluation, but the book continues far beyond this simplistic beginning. It encourages the reader to look beyond the function of a piece—to open his own "mind's eye," to expand his knowledge, and to reach for a deeper understanding of the creative spirit within each example. Albert Sack gives us not only the challenge but the opportunity to look at, to absorb, and to critically synthesize specific components within a particular object.

The introduction to this book is a clear revelation of the author's concepts and intentions to be addressed. The text and illustrations are manifestations of his discriminating eye, his vast knowledge, and, most importantly, of his deep love and regard both for the objects themselves, and for their creators. His enthusiastic respect for American furniture design pervades every page, and the reader will eagerly await each next set of gradations.

The New Fine Points of Furniture: Early American will no doubt join the first version as an essential treatise of the American decorative arts field. Albert Sack has given us all a very special gift. I would like to personally thank him for his contribution of this book to the field, for the opportunity to work with him on it, for always freely giving his knowledge to others and being a teacher of MASTERPIECE quality, and, especially, for being my friend. Knowing the many, many collectors, dealers, and scholars who share my sentiments, it is with sincere gratitude, honor and humility that I write this foreword.

Deanne D. Levison

INTRODUCTION

T his book is an extension of *Fine Points of Furniture: Early American,* published by Crown Publishers in 1950. That edition was based on the premise that the standards used in judging an American antique were in direct ratio to the relative quality of its form, integration, proportion, and craftsmanship. It also maintained that these standards were more important in grading a piece than its rarity, relative age within a period, history, documentation, or labels. *Fine Points I* demonstrated its thesis by showing pieces similar in type but varying in quality, using the designations GOOD, BETTER, BEST. GOOD was a kind designation for unsuccessful design, BETTER represented an item of reasonable competence but with a design flaw, BEST represented an item of successful design that ran the gamut from a basic piece above criticism to great masterpieces, with no categories to accommodate the distinction. There was nothing new about the concept; it was this rating premise on which Israel Sack depended throughout his career and which, we, his sons, have followed. The premise has proven useful in book form, not only to the beginning collector, but even to some advanced collectors, dealers, and scholars in establishing guidelines of taste and eliminating much of the decorative art terminology and technical verbiage that often confuses collectors and students trying to develop connoisseurship in this field.

It is now over forty years later, and the book has been printed more than twenty times with no revision except a change in the cover. I felt it was time to further develop its thesis in a new expanded volume, which American furniture as a recognized important art form deserves. Crown Publishers was more than enthusiastic about the need for this book, and my wife, Shirley, encouraged me to take on the project, which she gave the nickname "Jaws II."

For a long time I have realized that the criteria of GOOD, BETTER, BEST did not adequately expand the concepts that time and the developments within this field have made apparent to me. It is confining to equate a simple scrolled mirror that is merely beyond criticism with a masterpiece such as the Ten Eyck mirror (page 227). Therefore, to accommodate the successful artistic achievement reached by some inspired and gifted artisans in the colonies, I have added the two categories of SUPERIOR and MASTERPIECE. SUPERIOR represents the successful form that reaches beyond competence to the level of artistic brilliance within its medium and surpasses in excellence and creative skills the majority of its contemporaries. MASTERPIECE is defined by

Webster as a "supreme achievement." A MASTERPIECE, properly designated, transcends the bounds of the era or even the field of art it represents. It joins the ranks of the universal art of all eras. It is part of the "Arts Hall of Fame." But right away we run into a problem. What about pieces called SUPERIOR? Is that a lesser term? Most SUPERIOR pieces are MASTERPIECES, all MASTERPIECES are SUPERIOR. Some MASTERPIECES are more inspired than others. Some BETTER pieces deserve to be called BEST because sometimes the design flaws are minor and the overall effect of the piece is highly desirable. Some BEST pieces have design flaws, but not enough, in the critic's opinion, to take them out of the BEST category. The lesson is that there are many more than five categories and that all categorization is rigid and subject to interpretation and debate. This debate, however, is stimulating and is what the book is trying to accomplish. I do expect that some categories will be challenged; some represent very hard choices.

The basic criterion for explaining the difference between American and English furniture was defined in *Fine Points I*. That book developed the thesis that ornament dominated English furniture masterpieces—the form was supplementary to the ornament. In America, with no long history of resident royalty and palaces or grand manor houses of dukes and earls, superfluous grandeur was not of principal concern in furniture design. Perhaps the same psychological factors that, in the late eighteenth century, resulted in the creed "to form a more perfect union and to establish domestic tranquillity" were the same principles that led to the American preference for quality of line and proportion over ornamentation. Our finest craftsmen developed furniture forms with skillful restraint to a degree unsurpassed in England or France in the eighteenth century. English furniture was broad and emphasized the horizontal. Americans came to love the vertical proportion. As a result, unique forms were developed here that were unknown in England, such as the bonnet-and-scroll-top highboy and the compact block-front furniture of New England.

Note that not all American furniture stresses the vertical emphasis and not all English furniture emphasizes the horizontal, but the general distinction is most often valid. Israel Sack expressed it best when asked how he distinguished an American piece from an English prototype and he replied, "That's easy. By its accent." He also said, "Nelson's monument is of the greatest importance in Trafalgar Square. Bunker Hill Monument is equally important on Breed's Hill in Charlestown. But if you transposed Nelson's monument to Breed's Hill, it would lose all its significance and vice versa."

In more recent years, a very important new thesis has been developed by John Kirk in his book *American Furniture and the British Tradition*. Kirk spent years in England studying source prototypes for American furniture forms. He discovered and proved that the finest

American furniture did not directly derive its source from London or court furniture, but rather from the simpler country furniture of towns and small cities away from London. In demonstrating, for the first time, the close relationship between our urban furniture and the simpler rural furniture of England, it became more logical to compare our achievements with the domestic English counterparts. There is no question that the artisans who immigrated from Europe captured the American spirit of simplicity and fine craftsmanship that far outshone the creations of their domestic English rivals. Thus it is unnecessary to argue the relative merits of American masterpieces with English or London masterpieces. Each are superb and unrivaled in their own mediums.

This book has several comparisons of American SUPERIOR or MASTERPIECE pieces with English domestic pieces—the purpose is obviously not to demean or criticize English furniture where it succeeded the best but to show how American craftsmen developed form and line to a degree unparalleled by any decorative arts group. Also, a few English masterpieces will be compared to American masterpieces to show what each achieved using different, but equally superb, artistic models. It has been an uphill struggle in the antiques field to prove to connoisseurs the importance and uniqueness of American decorative arts, and the most difficult thing has been to prove that we were creators, not just imitators of our English forebears.

The stature of the American antique furniture field has increased enormously in the forty years since *Fine Points I* was written. The Metropolitan Museum reconstructed the American Wing, which is now one of the most popular exhibits in that great museum. Colonial Williamsburg opened a museum of American decorative arts. Miss Ima Hogg donated her collection to the city of Houston—it became the Bayou Bend Museum and is now a training ground for curators and a mecca for scholars west of the Mississippi. Clement Conger devoted himself with the zeal of the saints of old and the persuasive powers of a Thomas Paine to complete the White House Collection and establish the Diplomatic Reception Rooms of the State Department that represent for America what Versailles does for France. Visitors from nations around the world who come to Washington can now gain a new conception of our rich American artistic heritage.

The Museum of Early Southern Decorative Arts in Winston-Salem was established as a result of the dedication of Frank Horton and his loyal staff to reveal the important contributions of southern artisans. The research facilities established in the museum have no superiors and few equals in completeness and scholarly documentation.

The High Museum of Atlanta has formed a smaller, but outstanding, collection of masterpieces of eighteenth-century American furniture and an important collection of nineteenth-century furniture forms. The Dallas Museum purchased the Charles L. Bybee Collection of American furniture in 1985 and made it the nucleus of their newly formed American section. In 1988 the Art Institute of Chicago had a major expansion and, led by the efforts of curator Milo Naeve, has become one of the most active museums in acquisitions of American furniture masterpieces. The space allotted to American decorative arts has more than doubled, with vastly improved installations for their display. Significant developments or improvements have taken place at other museums in Milwaukee and Richmond, and at the Museum of Fine Arts, Boston. In the 1930s and 1940s, when Maxim Karolik was forming his collection, and even in the 1950s, American decorative arts holdings at the Museum of Fine Arts, Boston, were under the administration of Far Eastern Art.

There have been major exhibitions of American decorative arts that have established the new stature of American furniture. The National Gallery of Art in Washington has had two exhibits of American furniture—one in 1979 honoring the fiftieth anniversary of the Girl Scout Loan Exhibition of 1929 and one in 1986–1987 featuring American furniture from the George and Linda Kaufman Collection. In 1976 the Victoria and Albert Museum in London in conjunction with Yale University gave American furniture the high honor of a joint exhibition of American furniture masterpieces to honor our Bicentennial. Philadelphia, Baltimore, Boston, Providence, and Newport have all held major exhibits of furniture and decorative arts from their respective centers. Scholarly books and publications have abounded and discoveries in regional identifications and documentation have refined the scholarship greatly.

Study programs, fellowship programs, and curatorial training grounds have been established at Yale under the inspired leadership of the late Charles Montgomery and Dr. Patricia Kane. Winterthur Museum, the Museum of Early Southern Decorative Arts, Boston University, and others also have first-rate programs. Los Angeles County Museum in conjunction with the Metropolitan Museum of Art held a major exhibit of rococo American furniture in 1992. This book provides a bibliography of selected literature on the field published since 1950. In tandem with the new recognition and enthusiasm for American antiques, furniture prices, as well as the scope of collecting, rose dramatically. The prices rose in most major categories in ratios that rivaled the French and the American Impressionist and Hudson Valley paintings. The rise began in the 1960s abetted by the inflationary growth of the country and the establishment of a new and growing affluent middle and upper class. The clean lines and taste of the newly publicized American furniture appealed to growing numbers in this new group and new collectors appeared to compete on all levels.

The year 1950 marked the Norvin Green sale at which Israel Sack, Inc., bought a secretary desk for $6,750 and sold it for around $10,000. We have recently offered over one million dollars for that secretary. There were scores of outstanding pieces in that sale—most have become worth twenty-five to fifty times their cost since 1950. The 1960s was the era of collectors such as Lansdell Christie and Stanley Stone. Miss Ima Hogg came into the market to complete her collection. Mr. and Mrs. Charles Bybee began in the 1950s to form the superb collection now owned by the Dallas Museum of Art. The block-front secretary masterpiece Mrs. Bybee purchased from Israel Sack, Inc., in 1957 has been valued at about fifty times its cost to the Bybees. The Philadelphia piecrust table which our firm sold to Ray Hansen of Grosse Pointe for $15,000 was the first piece to bring one million dollars at auction. The strange, but typical, phenomenon was that as prices rose dramatically, new and more affluent collectors were drawn into this field in which it had become respectable to collect. No longer were collectors of American antique furniture considered eccentric.

The 1970s made the values of the 1960s seem infinitesimal. The outstanding collections formed by a considerable group of discriminating and venturesome private collectors dominated the masterpiece level of acquisitions. But an even larger group recognized the growing rarity of our beautiful Queen Anne and fine-line Chippendale furniture and avidly collected it as art forms. This furniture had been affordable and plentiful in the

1960s and 1970s, but prices began to escalate on the finer examples to the art level they always deserved. Graceful Queen Anne tea tables, lowboys, highboys, delightful little Philadelphia birdcage candlestands, Queen Anne side chairs and wing chairs, and many other simpler but beautiful unadorned creations rose twenty to fifty times their previous values and in turn went from plentiful to scarce. Thus the Queen Anne highboy and lowboy shown on page 184 was sold to Joseph Hirschhorn by Israel Sack, Inc., in 1957 for $10,000. We repurchased the combination in the 1980s for over $200,000. In the 1980s American collecting was in a pricing dimension never dreamed of in the 1970s. It began an era where at least several masterpieces have brought over one million dollars. Strangely, or not so strangely, today there are many more collectors watching for the scarce masterpiece to come on the market, even at these new price levels, than there were ten or fifteen years ago when prices were a fraction of those presently seen.

Since I wrote *Fine Points I*, scholarship and decorative arts terminology have become very sophisticated and precise. A highboy has become a high chest, a lowboy a dressing table, a Martha Washington chair a lolling chair, a bureau a chest-of-drawers, a kneehole desk a bureau table. Some of this new terminology I can accept; some I cannot live with. I was brought up calling a high chest a highboy, a dressing table a lowboy. I have called them highboys and lowboys and bureaus for the fifty-odd years I have been in the business. Just about all my dealer and collector friends call them highboys and lowboys. With apologies to all the decorative arts and museum colleagues I respect and admire, I think I will die calling them highboys and lowboys, as I do in this book. Perhaps we can call these terms popularizations or vernacular expressions, but they seem to me to be simple and descriptive.

The same is true of the arbitrary assignment of period—Queen Anne, Chippendale, et cetera. Just as GOOD, BETTER, et cetera, are each too rigid a boundary to be consistent, so, too, are assignations of period to narrowed circas. After all, craftsmen did not decide to stop making Chippendale furniture on December 31, 1780, and begin making only Hepplewhite or Federal on January 1, 1781. Formal urban Queen Anne furniture forms were popular right up to the Revolution, and many examples of pure "Queen Anne" form were made while the Chippendale era was in full bloom. In fact, particularly in Massachusetts centers, pad-foot chairs, tables, highboys, and lowboys outnumber claw-and-ball-foot examples by at least twenty to one. Should we then give a circa for Queen Anne furniture as 1730–1785? Hardly. Often there are two style influences in one piece. The distinction must be arbitrarily chosen; it is usually whatever influence the main thrust of the design depicts. A Goddard or Townsend highboy usually has claw and ball front feet and pad rear feet. Should we call the front Chippendale and the rear Queen Anne? One solution is not to use any period designations at all, but then we are again back to the vernacular. I think a designation of period is useful.

Finally, there is a problem with dating the style of furniture. Some very wonderful pieces were made in areas outside the big centers, with much expertise and quality. Many smaller centers and towns in New Hampshire, Connecticut and the Connecticut Valley, Chester County, and Lancaster, for example, produced pieces exhibiting earlier influences long after the general circas associated with those periods had past. Thus we know that many Connecticut Queen Anne highboys, lowboys, secretaries, et cetera, were produced between 1750–1800. If we designate their circa 1750–1780 we may be narrowing too much, but the main point is they are period pieces and should be judged for their merit. The placement of comparisons in this book, therefore, is not based on progression of dates, but rather by the relation of form. Thus we can have a highboy made in 1780 preceding one made in 1750 because its design serves to fit into the framework of the thesis we are developing.

Measurements have been included in this book when they were available. Therefore, not all pieces will have measurements and some measurements will be incomplete. But we felt that it would be useful to furnish whatever measure-

ments were possible to include. Measurements follow certain patterns. On a case piece, such as a secretary, highboy, slant-top desk, chest-on-chest, et cetera, the measurement is across the case or the lower case. On a piece with a top board, such as a lowboy, bureau, or sideboard, the measurement is the width and depth of the top. The height is always the total height, to the top of the finial if there is one. Side chairs are measured only by height, armchairs by height and width across arms, if available.

The English comparisons are generally not graded because the criteria we are applying are based on standards of relative merit of American furniture.

An astute collector who has long departed from the scene was Lou Brooks of Marshall, Michigan. Lou had a rhyme that I think sums up the uniqueness of American furniture. "Rich, but without show, plain but with a glow." I cannot let this book go to print without a tribute to my father, Israel Sack, who loved the spirit of American furniture and, more important, was a devotee of the genuine. I can remember when my father went to Plymouth to buy the Priscilla Alden cupboard. The price was right, but the drawers in the base had been converted to doors and my father would not buy it. Today it is in Pilgrim Hall and is a priceless heirloom. Israel Sack loved history, he loved Pilgrim furniture, but above all, he loved purity. And the legacy he left us all is inspirational.

ISRAEL SACK:
A TRIBUTE

The stature that American antique furniture holds, as reflected in this book and all recent literature of the field, depends in large part to the contributions of my father, Israel Sack. I feel privileged to have had the opportunity, along with my two brothers, to carry on his tradition of demonstrating to Americans and to the world the importance and creative genius of our colonial craftsmen.

In 1953 I prepared a tribute to Israel Sack on his fifty years in the field titled "Israel Sack: A Record of Service, 1903-1953". In it is a quote from Hayword A. Ablewhite, Chief Curator, The Henry Ford Museum: "To me, the outstanding fact in your career has been that you came to this country as a poor immigrant boy and acquired during the last fifty years a very wonderful understanding of the spirit that produced America. This I know, of course, has been duplicated many times by others, but certainly none has done it to a greater degree." Maxim Karolik, who gave his superb collection of American furniture to the Museum of Fine Arts, Boston, wrote, "You were among the very few dealers who helped the select few among collectors to raise American furniture from the antiquarian level to the status of art."

The theme of this book—that we achieved in line and form with understatement what England and France achieved in ornamentation and magnificence—was brought into focus for me, as well as the Americana field, by Israel Sack.

CHAIRS

BETTER

Pilgrim Carver armchair, probably Connecticut, circa 1680–1700 (left). The merit of Carver chairs is in direct ratio to the diameter of the posts. The more massive chairs are considered earlier and more in the Elizabethan tradition. The chairs are also rated by the quality of the turnings. This chair does not rate high on either count.

Ht: 40½" Wd: 24"   *Whereabouts unknown*

SUPERIOR

Pilgrim Carver armchair, Massachusetts, circa 1650–1700 (right). This chair has the weight associated with earlier models and also exhibits fine turnings.

Ht: 43¾" Wd: 23"   *Private collection*

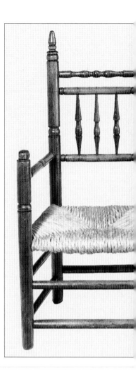

MASTERPIECE

Pilgrim Carver armchair, Massachusetts, circa 1650–1680. This superb massive chair has the greatest turned spindles and finials. It has few, if any, rivals in the Carver group. An early settler would hardly argue with a Pilgrim governor seated in this chair.

Ht: 45" Wd: 23½"
Wadsworth Athenaeum, Hartford, Connecticut
Wallace Nutting Collection
Gift of J. Pierpont Morgan

BETTER

William and Mary banister-back armchair with carved Prince of Wales crest, Massachusetts, circa 1710–1740. Although this is an important example, every element except perhaps the side stretchers is surpassed by the SUPERIOR chair. The arms are flat and shapeless and the proportion is not as stately. The outline of the banisters, the crest carving, and the turning of the frontal stretcher are relatively unrefined, although the side and rear stretchers are of the highest quality.

Whereabouts unknown

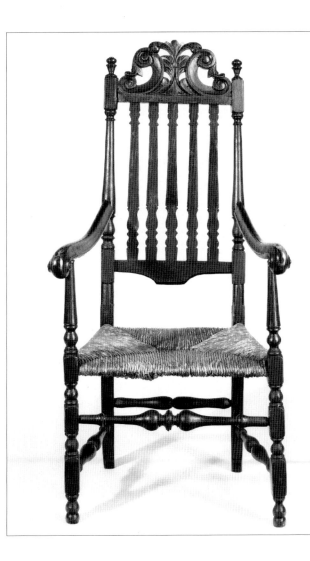

SUPERIOR

William and Mary banister-back armchair with carved Prince of Wales crest, Massachusetts, circa 1710–1740. A superbly designed, stately chair. The finely molded serpentine arms end in scrolled terminals. The carving of the crest and the execution of the turnings are top grade. It is interesting to note that the banister outlines follow the turnings of the stiles on both chairs.

Ht: 47⅞" Wd: 24⅛"
The Museum of Fine Arts, Houston,
The Bayou Bend Collection
Gift of Miss Ima Hogg

BETTER

Pilgrim slat-back armchair, New England, circa 1690–1720 (left). Although this chair has no basic design flaws, the thinness of the posts is not an asset in chairs of this form.

Whereabouts unknown

MASTERPIECE

Pilgrim slat-back armchair, Connecticut, circa 1650–1700. This is the king of the mushroom armchairs. It excels from every standpoint: the massiveness and quality of the turnings, the power of the mushroom terminals and the turned sloping arms, and the exceptional arch-outlined slats. The painted surface has survived many generations and is rare and priceless to find on a chair of this importance.

Ht: 42" Wd: 26"
Collection of Mr. and Mrs. Israel E. Liverant

BEST

Pilgrim slat-back armchair, Massachusetts, circa 1690–1710. A fine chair with bolder turnings and impressive mushroom terminals intact.

Ht: 46½" Wd: 26"   *Private collection*

BETTER

Queen Anne armchair, Rhode Island, circa 1740–1760. The chair is well crafted but has a heavy, squarish appearance caused by the breadth of the seat and the shortness of the back.

Ht: 42½" Wd: 29¾"

COURTESY OF CHRISTIE'S

MASTERPIECE

Queen Anne walnut armchair, Newport, Rhode Island, circa 1740–1760. The tall, stately proportions and brilliant blending of curved elements distinguish this outstanding model. Only a few such New England examples rival their highly developed Philadelphia counterparts. The sinuous arms of this chair connect with the rounded stiles into blocked panels, which are one piece with the stiles.

Ht: 42½" Wd: 31"   Private collection

PHOTOGRAPH: ISRAEL SACK, INC.

IRISH

Queen Anne mahogany armchair with shaped flat stretchers, Ireland, circa 1730–1760. This is an excellent comparison to depict the different emphasis exhibited in finely modeled understated chairs from two continents. This graceful Irish chair obviously served as a prototype and as an inspiration for the Philadelphia model. In fact, Philadelphia Queen Anne forms were influenced more by Irish designs than by those of London. This chair is broad and low, emphasizing the horizontal. The bowed, or horseshoe, seat is of fatter contour and does not have the spring of its Philadelphia counterpart, nor do the arm supports have the subtle contouring.

COURTESY OF JOHN KIRK, ILLUSTRATED IN HIS *AMERICAN FURNITURE AND THE BRITISH TRADITION TO 1830* (KNOPF, 1982).

Rear detail: This dramatizes the powerful but contained thrust of the incurvate arm as well as the skillful sculpting of the back. The chamfered edges of the splat create the silhouette effect of the frontal view.

AMERICAN: MASTERPIECE

Queen Anne walnut armchair, Philadelphia, circa 1740–1760. A superb sculptural entity achieved with no ornament. Each element flows into the other without interruption. Note how the scooped armrests mold into the rear stiles; also note the shaping of the arm support as it flows into the arm. The back outline springs like a taut bow as does the bell-shaped seat. The scooping of the armrest above and below creates a knife-blade effect.

Ht: 41" Wd: 24" at seat
Museum of Fine Arts, Boston

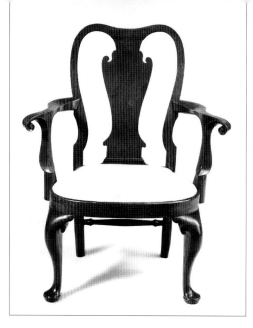

BETTER

Queen Anne walnut armchair with knuckle arm terminals, Philadelphia, circa 1740–1760. The best features of this chair are the finely modeled arms and incurvate arm supports. Comparison with the MASTERPIECE chair shows the inferior outline of the splat and the simplistic crest with no outlining. The heavy knee could use "plastic surgery."

Ht: 40¼" Wd: 32" across arms
Whereabouts unknown
PHOTOGRAPH: ISRAEL SACK, INC.

MASTERPIECE

Queen Anne walnut armchair with knuckle arm terminals and intaglio knee carving, attributed to William Savery, Philadelphia, circa 1740–1760. A study in mastery of the curvilinear formation. The outline of the vase-shaped splat is typical of the best models; the crest rail has a scribed line border and a modeled yoke center. The balloon, or horseshoe, seat frame has a tighter, more bowed curve, and the finely modeled legs have a lambrequin knee carving with well-defined drake feet. The result is beyond criticism. The chair descended in the family of Caspar Wistar of Salem, New Jersey.

Ht: 41½"   Private collection

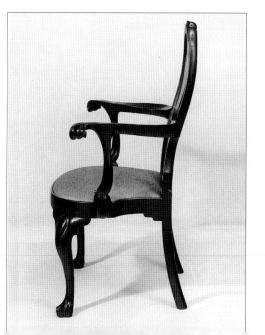

Profile view: This shows the effectiveness of the serpentine curve of the back and adds another dimension to the fine curvilinear composition. This view is rarely shown in illustrations and is often overlooked in judging the stature of Queen Anne chairs.

BETTER

Queen Anne walnut armchair with scrolled voluted splat, Philadelphia, **circa 1750–1770.** The finely modeled arms and the arm supports are of the finest quality. The failures of the back begin with a squat proportion, causing the important scrolled splat to be broad and heavy. The crest has scrolled voluted ears but nothing between the ears, like some people.

Whereabouts unknown

MASTERPIECE

Queen Anne walnut armchair with scrolled voluted splat, Philadelphia, **circa 1750–1770.** This magnificent armchair completes what the BETTER chair failed to accomplish. It lifts and slenderizes the beautiful splat and back, completing it with a spring to the bowed stiles and a shell-carved motif between the voluted ears.

Ht: 42" Wd: 31¾" across arms
Private collection
PHOTOGRAPH: ISRAEL SACK, INC.

ENGLISH:
MASTERPIECE

Queen Anne transitional armchair, English, circa 1730–1750. The broad, horizontal proportion of this chair is in keeping with the massive scale of contemporary London interiors. The form itself, however, is supplementary to its magnificent ornament, the work of a master carver. The cabriole leg, with relatively short thigh and ankle, has a broad knee that serves as a background for the ambitious carved detail.

Courtesy of Metropolitan Museum of Art
Kennedy Fund, 1918

AMERICAN:
MASTERPIECE

Queen Anne transitional armchair, Philadelphia, circa 1760–1770. The eye is drawn to the compact dynamism of the form as a whole. The carving serves as an accent and does not dominate the chair's composition. The integration of a variety of planes of curves into a harmonious unit is a tour de force. The emphasis is on the vertical, or slender, proportion accentuated by the height of the cabriole legs and the arced bow of the crest rail. The interplay of the scrolled volutes on the crest rail, splat, arm terminals, and knee returns helps hold the composition together. Note also the spring to the bow of the stiles and seat frame. The cabriole leg has a higher knee, longer ankle and thigh, and more of a bend—characteristics found on most American cabriole leg chairs that distinguish them from their English counterparts.

Ht: 44" Wd: 33¼" across arms
Courtesy of Metropolitan Museum of Art

BETTER

Queen Anne walnut side chair, Philadelphia, circa 1740–1760. A stately chair that suffers only from too much fat in the knee.

Whereabouts unknown

SUPERIOR

Queen Anne walnut side chair, Philadelphia, circa 1740–1760. A fine example with undulating stiles. Note the spring of the bow of the horseshoe seat. The stiles and the crest rail are outlined by a scribed line border.

Ht: 42¼"   Israel Sack, Inc.

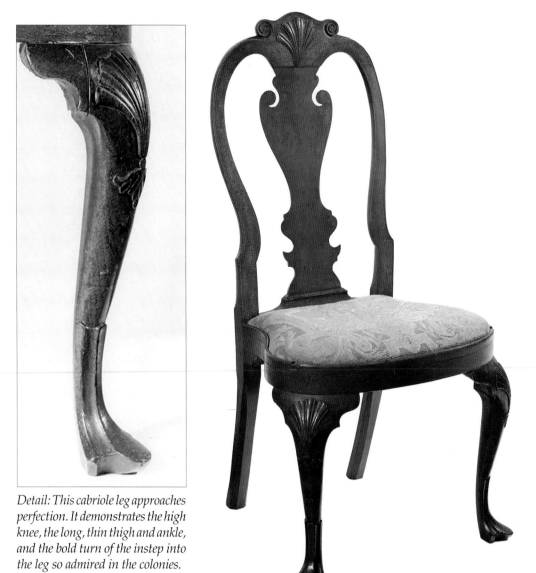

Detail: This cabriole leg approaches perfection. It demonstrates the high knee, the long, thin thigh and ankle, and the bold turn of the instep into the leg so admired in the colonies.

AMERICAN: MASTERPIECE

Queen Anne walnut side chair, Philadelphia, circa 1740–1760. This artisan reached the acme of perfection of grace and symmetry in the Philadelphia chair form. The chair's component parts illustrate its rare beauty: Note the magnificent slenderness of the shell and floral-carved knee and thigh and the spooning of the ankle as it turns into the stockinged drake feet, the tautness of the compass, or balloon-seat frame, and the spring of the bowed crest rail. The chair's beauty is enhanced by its undisturbed original aspect. The owner, J. R. Grove, was so proud of his masterpiece he branded his name into the seat frame. Another chair of this set is in the Bayou Bend Museum in Houston.

Ht: 42"   Private collection

ENGLISH

Queen Anne walnut side chair, English, circa 1720–1740 (right). A rural example fashioned by an average craftsman. Its simple lines, but not its finesse, come closer to American forms than the great London examples. Note the weak curve of the cabriole leg, the simplicity of the stretchers, and the squared outline of the seat frame.

Whereabouts unknown

AMERICAN:
SUPERIOR

Queen Anne walnut side chair, Newport, Rhode Island, circa 1740–1760 (left). This and the English counterpart have rounded stiles and crest and c-scrolled marginal carved knees, but that is where the similarity ends. In this example, skilled craftsmanship is shown in the curve of the cabriole leg, the bow of the horseshoe-shaped seat frame, the well-turned stretchers, and the outline of the vase-shaped splat.

Ht: 40¼"
Collection of Suzanne and Norman Hascoe

AMERICAN:
MASTERPIECE

Queen Anne walnut side chair attributed to Job Townsend, Newport, Rhode Island, circa 1740–1760. A superb blending of curved elements into a uniform composition. The taut bow formed by the arced stiles and the crest rail is a tour de force. The cyma-shaped apron of the horseshoe-shaped seat frame is fashioned from three-inch stock. The typical Newport flat stretchers and c-scrolled marginal carving complete an exciting composition. A set of chairs of this design was made by Job Townsend for the Eddy family in 1743.

Ht: 40¼"
Formerly Israel Sack, Inc.
(whereabouts unknown)

BETTER

Queen Anne walnut balloon-seat side chair, Rhode Island, circa 1740–1760. An adequate but uninspired version of the New York/Newport Queen Anne chair. The simplistic splat and weak claw and ball feet compare unfavorably with the finer models.

Whereabouts unknown

PHOTOGRAPHIC ARCHIVES, NATIONAL GALLERY OF ART

SUPERIOR

Queen Anne mahogany balloon-seat side chair with shell-carved crest, New York or Newport, Rhode Island, circa 1740–1760. Assigning regional origin to a chair that has elements of both New York and Newport designs is a problem. Both centers adopted each other's motifs and elements. Usually the assignation is made by the preponderance of motifs and formation typical of one or the other center; in this case the back is typically Newport, the seat and base are typically New York. In any event, it is an outstanding chair, stately in proportion, with a finely shaped base, splat, and a bold, carved convex shell.

Ht: 41"   Collection of Martin Crane

BETTER

Queen Anne walnut transitional side chair, Delaware Valley, circa 1750–1770 (right). This transitional form became popular in the Delaware Valley area beginning in the 1740s and continuing to around the Revolutionary era. This is an average example of pleasing proportion and a competent vase-shaped splat. However, the cabriole legs lack the bend and the finely modeled drake feet of the following examples.

Whereabouts unknown

SUPERIOR

Queen Anne transitional side chair, Philadelphia, circa 1760–1770 (right). A well-modeled chair of stately proportion. Skillful workmanship is evident in the vase splat outlining, the shaping of the crest rail with its carved shell center, and the fine cabriole legs.

Ht: 40½"   Israel Sack, Inc.

BEST

Queen Anne walnut transitional side chair, Delaware Valley, circa 1750–1770 (left). The pleasing curve of the cabriole leg adds an aesthetic dimension to this popular model.

Whereabouts unknown

ENGLISH

Chippendale mahogany pad-foot side chair, England, circa 1750–1780 (left). This perfectly competent chair is shown to emphasize the predominance of the horizontal proportion in English models.

PHOTOGRAPHIC ARCHIVES, NATIONAL GALLERY OF ART

AMERICAN: BEST

Chippendale mahogany pad-foot side chair, Massachusetts, circa 1760–1780 (right). The American preference for the vertical proportion is demonstrated when compared to the English model. The cabriole leg has more lift and its curve is accentuated by the ridged knee. The ribbed instep is an effective touch. The absence or presence of stretchers depended on the preference of the client.

Ht: 38"   Israel Sack, Inc.

AMERICAN: SUPERIOR

Chippendale mahogany pad-foot side chair, Massachusetts, circa 1760–1780. Superior modeling, subtle refinements, and a rare state of preservation lifts a standard model to an exalted stature. The raising of the knee and the smooth flow of the inner ankle and thigh surpass the competent leg of the BEST chair. The strapwork of the splat intersects the diamond in a three-dimensional effect. The leather seat is original.

Ht: 36½"   Private collection

BEST

Chippendale walnut balloon-seat side chair, Massachusetts, circa 1760–1770. The balloon seat and the base could be transposed on a Queen Anne chair, showing that the popularity of the earlier form had endured throughout the pre-Revolutionary era. The crest rail and splat are less developed than the same elements on the other two chairs.

Ht: 38½"   Israel Sack, Inc.
PHOTOGRAPH: ISRAEL SACK, INC.

SUPERIOR

Chippendale mahogany balloon-seat side chair, Newport, Rhode Island, circa 1760–1780. The competence of the crest rail, with its molded ears and cross-hatched center, is apparent as is the superior delineation of the interlaced splat. Newport Chippendale chairs of this quality are quite rare.

Ht: 38"   Whereabouts unknown
PHOTOGRAPH: ISRAEL SACK, INC.

MASTERPIECE

Chippendale mahogany balloon-seat side chair, Massachusetts, circa 1760–1780. A truly magnificent specimen showing the balance and mastery of proportion so often achieved by Massachusetts artisans. The cabriole leg, with rounded knee, integrates well with the curve of the bell-shaped seat and ends in a finely sculptured claw and ball foot. The adequate breadth and fine trim of the back combine to form a harmonious unit.

Ht: 38"
Yale University Art Gallery
Mabel Brady Garvan Collection

WHAT IS A SHELL WORTH?

BETTER

Chippendale mahogany claw-and-ball-foot side chair, Newport, Rhode Island, circa 1760–1780. This has all the elements of an important and rare model. The claw and ball foot relates to more developed examples of the Goddard-Townsend school. Yet, the ankles sag, the cabriole legs are angular, and the back lacks the finesse of refined modeling.

Ht: 38½"
Whereabouts unknown

SUPERIOR

Chippendale mahogany claw-and-ball-foot side chair, Boston, circa 1760–1780 (one of a pair). Superiority in every element over the Newport chair is evident. The crest rail has a rhythmic flow and integrates smoothly into the skillfully modeled scrolled and voluted splat. The cabriole leg has a perfect curve, accentuated by a ridged knee thinning to a "well-turned" ankle and ending in a finely sculptured claw and ball foot. To the less sophisticated collector, the Newport chair would be more desirable because it has a shell-carved crest and Goddard school claw and ball foot. To the connoisseur, the artistry achieved without adornment by the Massachusetts example places it in a higher category.

Currier Gallery of Art,
Manchester, New Hampshire
PHOTOGRAPH: ISRAEL SACK, INC.

ORNAMENT VS. FORM

GOOD

Chippendale mahogany side chair with pierced vase-shaped splat, North Shore Massachusetts, circa 1760–1785. The ambitious carved crest, splat, and knees adorn a chair with cramped proportions, a weak crest rail, and crudely formed legs and claw and ball feet.

Ht: 38½"   *Whereabouts unknown*

SUPERIOR

Chippendale mahogany side chair with pierced vase-shaped splat, Boston, circa 1760–1785. This model achieves in unadorned form what its counterpart attempts in ornament. The beautifully curved cabriole leg has a pointed knee to outline the curve and ends in a finely sculptured claw and ball foot. Superiority is also evident in the finely wrought splat and crest rail. It would be more valuable than that of its competitor, proving that successful form is more important than carving, unless that carving is on an equally competent form.

Ht: 37¾"
Society for the Preservation of
New England Antiquities
PHOTOGRAPH: RICHARD CHEEK

ENGLISH

Chippendale mahogany Gothic-splat side chair, England, circa 1750–1770. The thesis that our master craftsmen worked more closely from the English country models than from the London masterworks is strengthened by this comparison. The squared proportion contrasts to the verticality of the following Wharton chairs. The heavy knee is typically English, and the undulation of the crest rail is not matched by the plain apron. The turned stretchers are a carryover from the Queen Anne period.

Whereabouts unknown

PHOTOGRAPHIC ARCHIVES, NATIONAL GALLERY OF ART

AMERICAN: MASTERPIECE

Chippendale mahogany Gothic-splat side chair, Philadelphia, circa 1760–1780. One of a large set made for Joseph Wharton by Thomas Affleck. The perfection of the design of this outstanding chair is matched by the skill of the carver. The twin-arch apron unites brilliantly with the beautifully formed cabriole legs. The richly carved knee brackets are matched by the equally vibrant, three-dimensional ear carving.

Private collection

PHOTOGRAPH: ISRAEL SACK, INC.

Detail of back: The carved elements outline rather than dominate a superbly integrated composition.

BEST

Chippendale mahogany claw-and-ball-foot side chair with shell-carved ears, **Philadelphia, circa 1760–1780.** A pleasing example with six shells and a well-modeled interlaced splat with scrolled volutes. While competent in its own right, it cannot vie in stature with its MASTERPIECE counterpart.

Ht: 39½"   Whereabouts unknown

MASTERPIECE

Chippendale mahogany claw-and-ball-foot side chair with shell-carved ears, **attributed to Thomas Affleck, Philadelphia, circa 1760–1780 (one of a pair).** It is hard to find superlatives to describe the brilliance of this inspired creation. The shell-carved ears blossom to complete a rhythmic crest rail to which the scroll tips flanking the shell add a scintillating touch. The balance and integration are perfect. The carved knees and strapwork and the fluted stiles accent the composition. The original condition of this pair of chairs and the vibrant colors of the original needlepoint seats are superb.

Ht: 40½"
Collection of Erving and Joyce Wolf
PHOTOGRAPH: ISRAEL SACK, INC.

PAGE FROM ENGLISH FURNITURE
by Luke Vincent Lockwood (1909)

ENGLISH FURNITURE *of the XVII and XVIII CENTURIES*

PLATE XCIV

MAHOGANY SIDE CHAIR IN
CHIPPENDALE STYLE
(1740-1750)

A NOTHER varia-
tion of the concave
and long cyma curve is
shown in this chair. The
splat is carved to represent drapery and tassels, with an intertwined ribbon
effect in the center, a design very popular during this period. Across the
top of the rail of the back is carved a slight acanthus leaf tracery. The
legs are cabriole, terminating in bird's claw and ball feet, and the knees are
carved in an acanthus leaf design.

ENGLISH FURNITURE *of the XVII and XVIII CENTU*

PLATE X

MAHOGANY SIDE (
CHIPPENDALE .
(1740-1750)

T HIS chair
similar in
the preceding ex
worked out. The top rail is carved in an acanthus leaf design, belo
is drapery with three tassels. Below this is the ribbon effect, simila
in the preceding chair. The legs are cabriole, terminating in bir
and ball feet, and the knees are beautifully carved in leaf effect. T
of the back are fluted and reeded. This chair represents the perfe
this design. Number 17 is similar.

AMERICAN

ENGLISH

L uke Vincent Lockwood published a still-popular pioneering work on American furniture,
Colonial Furniture in America, in 1913. Few people know of an earlier work by Lockwood,
published in 1909, entitled *English Furniture.* It appears that Lockwood learned within four
years that some beautiful formal furniture was actually made in this country by our own
artisans. Imagine the strides we have made in this century in our regional and native
definitions. Above are two pages from the 1909 publication that show similar interpretations of the same model. In that publication, Lockwood considered both English.

Plate XCIV we now know shows a Philadelphia piece; Plate XCV shows an English example.
Lockwood considers the English chair superior due to richer carved elements. The two major
differences between American and English designs are clearly apparent here. The Philadelphia chair emphasizes the vertical, the graceful form dominates, and the carving serves as an
accent. The cabriole leg has a high knee, more thigh and ankle, and a more serpentine bend.
The English counterpart is broader, emphasizing the horizontal, and the knee encompasses
over half the cabriole to serve as a foil for the rich carving.

PHOTOGRAPHS: JAMES CONZO

ENGLISH

Chippendale mahogany claw-and-ball-foot side chair, England, circa 1755–1770. As with the English chair in Lockwood's book (Plate XCV), this example is broader and heavier than the Philadelphia example. The broader splat loses the tension and rhythm of its counterpart; the crest rail is relatively weak. Obviously, this interpretation is not the top level of English form (in fact, the illustration in Lockwood's book is superior), yet it clearly points out the vitally different styles of the two countries.

PHOTOGRAPHIC ARCHIVES, NATIONAL GALLERY OF ART

AMERICAN: MASTERPIECE

Chippendale mahogany claw-and-ball-foot side chair, Philadelphia, circa 1760–1780. This chair is closely related to the example in Lockwood's Plate XCIV. Despite the richness of the carved stiles and crest, the chair has a unity, with the competent carving serving to outline and accentuate the basic design. The strapwork splat is symphonic and shows the hand of a genius.

Whereabouts unknown

GOOD
(FOR NOTHING)

Chippendale Revival mahogany claw-and-ball-foot side chair, Philadelphia, circa 1880–1900. The 1876 celebrations of one hundred years of independence included exhibitions of eighteenth-century furniture forms. These exhibitions engendered a rash of Revival furniture imitating early forms, particularly Philadelphia Chippendale chairs. It is useful to illustrate one such piece. The sudden stiffening of the cabriole curve, the crude carving on the solid splat, and the stiff proportions make this example an obvious Revival piece. Some Revival or Centennial chairs follow the traditional form more closely and present an identification challenge to the experts.

Whereabouts unknown

Detail of carved back

SUPERIOR

Chippendale mahogany side chair, Philadelphia, circa 1760–1780. An outstanding example of superb proportion and brilliant distribution of carved elements. The tassel-carved crest with cartouche center, the acanthus-carved scrolled interlaced splat, and the cartouche carving above the knees are all essential to the design of the chair. Note the dramatic bend in the cabriole legs.

Dr. Warren Koontz

ENGLISH: MASTERPIECE

Chippendale mahogany claw-and-ball-foot side chair, London, circa 1750–1760 (one of a set of six). This magnificent creation epitomizes the supreme heights of London master craftsmanship, as well as the differences between the English and American counterparts. The emphasis here is on the superb carving, which dominates the composition. The eye is drawn first to the ornamentation; the form, though important, is supplementary to the carving. The horizontal proportion and the breadth of the chair are typical of English preference. The relatively short cabriole legs add to the horizontal emphasis.

Metropolitan Museum of Art

AMERICAN: MASTERPIECE

Chippendale mahogany claw-and-ball-foot side chair, Philadelphia, circa 1760–1775 (descended from David Deschler of Germantown). Both this and its English counterpart excel in carving. The scrolled and voluted ears bear some relationship, and on both, the knee carving is in bold relief. Yet here the similarity ends. In the Deschler chair, the form dominates the composition while the carving serves as an accent. There is not an iota of carving that is not essential to the development of the composition. The apron of the seat rail is formed of twin scribed, outlined arches, successfully solving the design problem of uniting the frame with the cabriole legs. Note the emphasis on the vertical proportion. The cabriole legs are tall with a high knee and more thigh and ankle than its English counterpart with a finely sculptured claw and ball foot.

Ht: 38½"
Formerly Israel Sack, Inc.
(whereabouts unknown)

BETTER

Chippendale mahogany tassel-back side chair, New York, circa 1760–1780. The relatively inept crest rail suffers in comparison to the superior Van Rensselaer model (below).

Whereabouts unknown

PHOTOGRAPHIC ARCHIVES, NATIONAL GALLERY OF ART

MASTERPIECE

Chippendale mahogany tassel-back side chair, New York, circa 1760–1780. This is one of the best designs produced by New York chairmakers and vies with some of the finer Philadelphia counterparts. The tassel-and-ruffle-carved splat is contained in a well-integrated composition. The acanthus-carved cabriole legs end in typical New York squared claw and ball feet. The form was a favorite of the prominent Van Rensselaer family, and more than one set was made for it.

Ht: 38½"
Collection High Museum of Art, Atlanta; purchased with funds from a supporter of the Museum, 1978.1000.16

BETTER

Chippendale cherry side chair, Connecticut, circa 1770–1780. A pleasant
but undistinguished chair with a simple, undeveloped crest and splat.

© 1974, Sotheby's, Inc.

SUPERIOR

Chippendale mahogany side chair, Boston, circa 1760–1780. The height of development of a standard model in a rare
state of preservation, retaining the original
leather seat and tacks. The molded legs and
stretchers, the fine interlaced splat with
scrolled volutes, and the excellent proportions make this chair a worthy specimen.

Ht: 38"   Metropolitan Museum of Art

GOOD

Chippendale walnut armchair with knuckle arm terminals, Philadelphia, circa 1760–1780. This chair serves as an excellent contrast to the SUPERIOR and MASTERPIECE examples. The splat is underdeveloped, the modeling of the arms and arm supports is relatively crude, and the cabriole legs lack the bend that appears on the other chairs. Obviously, this is a harsh condemnation of a nice chair with a character of its own, but its stature and value will never approach those of the SUPERIOR model.

Whereabouts unknown

SUPERIOR

Chippendale walnut armchair with knuckle arm terminals, Philadelphia, circa 1760–1780. An outstanding chair. The finely wrought elements blend together in perfect harmony. The armrests are chamfered to effect both thinness and strength; the molded undulating arm supports integrate smoothly into the arms. The fluted stiles and the carved cabochon shell centering the crest add to the chair's stature.

Ht: 40¾" Wd: 30½"
Diplomatic Reception Rooms,
United States Department of State

MASTERPIECE

Chippendale mahogany armchair with knuckle arm terminals, Philadelphia, circa 1760–1780. The art of a Philadelphia carver combines with a powerful, successful form to make one of the greatest Philadelphia Chippendale armchairs. This chair exudes virility and power with no sacrifice of fluency. The tassel-carved crest rail is outstanding. The scrolled knuckle terminals of the crest, the scrolled knuckle arm terminals, the scrolled volutes of the strapwork splat, and the volutes of the carved knee brackets knit the composition together. This magnificent chair, from the Leedom-Sharp family, was reportedly used by George Washington in Germantown. It belonged to Mrs. Sharp in California who, when Israel Sack tried to buy the chair from her, said, "Mr. Sack, I bet you hope I go broke so you can buy my chair." Israel Sack answered, "Mrs. Sharp, no self-respecting man wants to benefit from someone else's misfortune." Mrs. Sharp said, "Try me again in twenty-five years." Twenty-five years later we bought the chair from her son, and it is now in a private collection.

Ht: 39½" Wd: 31"   ***Private collection***

PHOTOGRAPH: ISRAEL SACK, INC.

ENGLISH

Chippendale mahogany claw-and-ball-foot side chair with diamond splat, England, circa 1750–1770 (left). A rural English example, certainly far from the best of this form produced in England. It is shown here to demonstrate how the simple American forms were produced by master craftsmen while the rural English forms, their closest prototypes, were generally fashioned by less skilled craftsmen.

© 1977, SOTHEBY'S, INC.

AMERICAN: BEST

Chippendale mahogany claw-and-ball-foot side chair with diamond splat, New York, circa 1760–1780 (right). A typical New York side chair of pleasing proportion. For whatever reason, New York pre-Revolutionary chairs are not as skillfully crafted as are comparable Philadelphia examples.

Ht: 38"
Formerly Israel Sack, Inc.
(whereabouts unknown)

AMERICAN: MASTERPIECE

Chippendale mahogany claw-and-ball-foot side chair with diamond splat, New York, circa 1760–1780. The ultimate in New York Chippendale expression. The beauty provided by the transitional horse-shoe-shaped seat frame, with its scrolled apron, makes one wonder why it was not used more often. The diamond splat is more three-dimensional than usual, and the crest rail has well-placed carving. The chair is one of a set; another example is at the Henry Francis du Pont Winterthur Museum.

Ht: 39½"
Yale University Art Gallery
Mabel Brady Garvan Collection

BETTER

Chippendale maple Gothic-splat side chair, New England or Philadelphia, circa 1760–1780 (left). The standard Gothic splat lacks the tasteful flare of the end bars seen on the following examples, and the crest lacks spring in the bowed outline.

Whereabouts unknown

PHOTOGRAPHIC ARCHIVES, NATIONAL GALLERY OF ART

BEST

Chippendale mahogany Gothic-splat side chair, Philadelphia, circa 1760–1780 (right). Though still a conventional chair, the floral c-scrolls outlining the crest and splat elements are refinements. The Gothic arch appears more three-dimensional, and the end bars have a more pronounced flare than the BETTER example.

© 1977, SOTHEBY'S, INC.

MASTERPIECE

Chippendale mahogany Gothic-splat side chair, one of a set of six signed by Samuel Walton, Philadelphia, circa 1760–1780. Rarely do signed examples reach the height of development that is attained by these six chairs. The refinement of the pierced corner brackets and the bead and reel centering the molded legs is matched by the molding of the stiles and crest rail.

Ht: 38"   Private collection

BEST

Chippendale mahogany armchair with knuckle arm terminals, Philadelphia, circa 1760–1785. A competent example with nicely modeled arms. The simple crest would be helped with beaded or carved trim, as seen on the SUPERIOR and MASTERPIECE examples.

Whereabouts unknown

PHOTOGRAPHIC ARCHIVES, NATIONAL GALLERY OF ART

SUPERIOR

Chippendale mahogany armchair with knuckle arm terminals, Philadelphia, circa 1760–1785. The highly arched bows of the crest rail add lift to the design. The incurvate arm supports and the scrolled brackets add stature.

© SOTHEBY'S, INC.

Detail: side view showing the exquisitely carved arm supports and terminals.

MASTERPIECE

Chippendale mahogany armchair made for Governor John Penn and attributed to Thomas Affleck, Philadelphia, circa 1760–1785. A study in symmetry that could be accomplished only by a genius. The scrolled beading of the arm supports sinuously flows into the delicately scrolled terminals. The fret design of the legs relates to the great Chew sofa in Cliveden, also by Affleck.

Ht: 39¾" Wd: 27"   Private collection

PHOTOGRAPH: ISRAEL SACK, INC.

BETTER

Chippendale walnut claw-and-ball-foot armchair, Philadelphia, circa 1760–1770. An otherwise fine chair is made less desirable by a short, low back and crudely outlined vase splat.

Whereabouts unknown
PHOTOGRAPHIC ARCHIVES, NATIONAL GALLERY OF ART

BETTER

Chippendale walnut claw-and-ball-foot armchair, Philadelphia, circa 1760–1770. Although this chair has some good features, particularly the finely modeled cabriole legs, apron, and crest, the back is too short and the nicely outlined splat too broad for perfect proportion. The stiff arms and arm supports lack the finesse of the SUPERIOR example.

Whereabouts unknown

SUPERIOR

Chippendale walnut claw-and-ball-foot armchair, Philadelphia, circa 1760–1770. A beautiful model from every standpoint—proportion, skill of modeling, and design. The reduction in the breadth of the splat gives a lighter appearance to the back, as does the refined sculpturing of the arms and exquisite arm supports. The perfectly formed cabriole legs have tensile strength, yet complement the slender effect of the composition.

Ht: 39" Wd: 29"
Collection of Mr. and Mrs. Arthur Levitt, Jr.

ENGLISH

Chippendale walnut or mahogany oval stool, England, circa 1750–1770 (one of a pair). An interesting comparison that illustrates the basic difference between English and American design, each great in its own sphere. This stool is choice and rare, with a distinct English emphasis. The boldly carved knees encompass two-thirds of the cabriole legs, dominating the composition.

© SOTHEBY'S, INC.

AMERICAN: MASTERPIECE

Chippendale mahogany oval stool, Philadelphia, circa 1760–1780. This outstanding rarity is one of less than a handful of American Chippendale stools. Note the different emphasis of the cabriole legs, with their high knees and longer ankles, in comparison to the English example. The acanthus carving blends into, rather than dominates, the composition, giving it unity.

Ht: 15⅝" Wd: 20⅜"
Courtesy Henry Francis du Pont
Winterthur Museum

GOOD

Hepplewhite cherry transitional arm-chair, Rhode Island, circa 1790–1810. A rural interpretation showing a lack of skill both in proportion and refinement in crafts-manship.

Whereabouts unknown
PHOTOGRAPH: JOHN HOPF

BEST

Hepplewhite mahogany transitional armchair, Rhode Island, circa 1780–1800. Descended in the family of Elbridge Gerry, signer of the Declaration of Independence from Massachusetts. This model exhibits every refinement the GOOD chair lacks. The splat is first quality, the stiles and crest have a good spring, the arms are nicely sculptured, and the molded arm supports and legs integrate into a pleasing composition.

Whereabouts unknown

BETTER

Hepplewhite mahogany transitional side chair, Connecticut or Rhode Island, circa 1780–1800. The splat with central carved urn is competent and typical of a large group from both states. The stiles lack the spring of the BEST chair and the legs are heavy for this form.

© 1977, SOTHEBY'S, INC.

SUPERIOR

Hepplewhite mahogany transitional side chair, Rhode Island, circa 1780–1800 (below). This finely carved urn and drapery splat is seen on a number of transitional and shield-back side chairs fashioned in Newport and Providence. Note the molded stiles and molded tapered legs and the graceful flow of the stiles into the crest rail.

Ht: 40"   *Private collection*

BEST

Hepplewhite mahogany transitional side chair, Connecticut, circa 1780–1800 (above). A fine specimen of grace and refinement. Note the spring of the bow of the stiles and crest rail, as well as the delicate stance of the serpentine seat frame and tapered legs.

© 1977, SOTHEBY'S, INC.

BETTER

Hepplewhite mahogany shield-back side chair, Salem, Massachusetts, circa 1780–1800 (left). The splat of three bars ending in carved tulip terminals is typical of the Salem school. The shape of the shield and the bowed members of the splat do not measure up to those of the SUPERIOR and MASTERPIECE comparisons.

Ht: 36½"   Israel Sack, Inc.

SUPERIOR

Hepplewhite mahogany shield-back side chair, Salem, Massachusetts, circa 1780–1800 (one of a pair) (right). The hand of a superior artisan is evident in the conformation of the molded shield and the smooth curve of the slats as they emanate from the carved crescent. The spade feet and the incurvate shape of the rear legs add to the chair's finesse. The horsehair seat cover is the original.

Ht: 38"   Israel Sack, Inc.

MASTERPIECE

Hepplewhite mahogany shield-back side chair, carved by Samuel Mc-Intire for Elias Haskett Derby, Salem, Massachusetts, circa 1780–1800. The typical Salem shield back encloses a superbly carved urn and drapery slat. The grape carving of the legs and the ebonized spade feet are also characteristics of the master carver of Salem.

Ht: 38⅜"
The Cleveland Museum of Art,
purchase from the J. H. Wade Fund, 62.125

ENGLISH

Hepplewhite mahogany shield-back side chair, England, circa 1780–1790. This chair by no means has the sophistication of a London chair, but it illustrates the English broad proportion and the use of frills in the splat which the colonial version brings down to essentials.

Whereabouts unknown

Detail of back.

SUPERIOR

Hepplewhite mahogany shield-back side chair, carving attributed to Samuel McIntire, Salem, Massachusetts, circa 1780–1800 (one of a pair). The vertical emphasis that distinguishes the American chair from its English prototype is apparent here. The outlines are strongly drawn and there is a unity and integrity to the composition. The detail shows the carving and star-punch background of a precision that indicates the hand of the great carver of Salem.

Ht: 38"   Private collection

BETTER-BEST

Hepplewhite mahogany shield-back armchair with spade feet, Baltimore, circa 1780–1800 (left). A pleasing chair of competent modeling. The splat bars are molded and flaring but uninspired.

Ht: 37¼"
Formerly Israel Sack, Inc.
(whereabouts unknown)

SUPERIOR

Hepplewhite mahogany inlaid shield-back armchair with spade feet, Baltimore, circa 1780–1800 (right). An inspired version. The typical Baltimore pierced splats have a central bellflower inlay and the serpentine veneered seat frame has an inlaid border. The arms have a nice spring and graceful arm support.

Ht: 39"   Private collection

BETTER-BEST

Sheraton mahogany racquet-back armchair, Virginia, circa 1800–1815 (left). Though Philadelphia influence is strong, the rural interpretation is apparent in the lack of development of the arms and the broad proportions. This chair assumes great importance due to its history of belonging to Richard Kidder Meade of Albemarle County, Virginia, who was George Washington's physician.

Ht: 36"   Virginia Governor's Mansion

SUPERIOR

Sheraton mahogany racquet-back armchair, Philadelphia, circa 1800–1815 (right). One of the many competent chairmakers operating in Philadelphia fashioned this finely modeled chair. Note the tightness of the composition and the carefully contoured arms.

Ht: 36"   Collection of Mrs. Max Adler

SUPERIOR-MASTERPIECE

Sheraton mahogany racquet-back armchair, attributed to John Aitken, Philadelphia, circa 1795–1810 (one of a set of twelve). This chair combines symmetry, fine proportion, and detail representing the finest Philadelphia had to offer. Its quality is hard to surpass in any colonial center. George Washington ordered a set of this design from John Aitken.

Ht: 37"   Private collection

© 1988, SOTHEBY'S, INC.

BETTER

Classical mahogany lyre-back side chair, Duncan Phyfe school, New York, circa 1810–1825 (one of a pair). The goats' legs with cloven hooves would be more suitable on a goat. The drapery-carved crest panel is an important feature, yet the acanthus-carved lyre lacks the finesse of the SUPERIOR model.

© 1977, SOTHEBY'S, INC.

SUPERIOR

Classical mahogany lyre-back side chair, attributed to Duncan Phyfe, New York, circa 1810–1820 (one of a pair). The superb craftsmanship, first-rank carving, and mastery of form that gives Duncan Phyfe his stature among America's master craftsmen is displayed in this chair. The tight-knit acanthus carving of the lyre and the acanthus and hairy paw–carved legs show the superiority to the BETTER model.

Ht: 32½"   Private collection

MASTERPIECE

Classical mahogany harp-back side chair, attributed to Duncan Phyfe, New York, circa 1810–1825.** The symmetry achieved by integrating the asymmetrical harp into a conventional frame is a brilliant achievement. The quality of the craftsmanship and selection of choice mahogany indicates the work of a master.

Ht: 32½"
Collection of Mr. and Mrs. Edward L. Stone

Detail of back. The complexity of the harp-back design limited its output to only a very few sets of this design.

BETTER

Queen Anne curly maple corner chair, Massachusetts, circa 1750–1760. The cabriole leg with its c-scrolled marginal borders and platformed pad foot is the best part of this chair. The deep aprons, the simple side and rear legs and the stiff back rate valid criticisms.

Ht: 32½"

COURTESY OF CHRISTIE'S

SUPERIOR

Queen Anne San Domingan mahogany corner chair, Salem, Massachusetts, circa 1750–1770 (descended in the Broughton family). The product of a master craftsman skilled in design integration and finished modeling. The aprons are gracefully curved; the side and rear legs have platformed disc feet; the splats and crest are of high quality.

Ht: 30¼" Wd: 28½" across arms
Private collection

BETTER

Queen Anne walnut corner chair with vase-shaped splats, Rhode Island, circa 1750–1770. This is a typical corner chair that suffers only by comparison with the SUPERIOR example. The pointed seat does not have the fluency of the comparative horseshoe seat. The turnings of the end legs, columns, and stretchers lack definition and the vase splats do not have the fullness or the ogival outlining of the vase splats.

Whereabouts unknown

SUPERIOR

Queen Anne walnut corner chair with vase-shaped splats, Rhode Island, circa 1740–1760. This chair is flawless in design, craftsmanship, and detail. The rounding of the knee blends with the rounded front of the seat frame, effecting a smooth integration. The turnings are competent and the side and rear legs end in well-modeled pad feet.

Ht: 31½" Wd: 29" across arms
Private collection

BETTER

Chippendale cherry corner chair with four cabriole legs, claw and ball feet, Connecticut, circa 1770–1780. While the general descriptions are similar, any relationship between this example and the following Goddard MASTERPIECE is purely coincidental. Compare the square seat to the horseshoe outlines of the other. The pierced splat is simplistic, and the balls of the feet are somewhat flattened.

Whereabouts unknown

Side view of opposite page.

MASTERPIECE

Chippendale mahogany corner chair with four cabriole legs, claw and ball feet, and incurvate arm supports, attributed to John Goddard and made for one of the Brown brothers of Providence, Rhode Island, circa 1760–1765. Just as the sculptors of ancient Greece applied their genius to masterpiece sculpture in marble, the great Newport masters carved sculptured masterpieces from San Domingan mahogany. No better evidence of their genius exists than in this sculpture in wood. What the great masters of other cultures achieved in complex ornamentation, this master achieved in form alone by uniting a series of at least five planes of curves into a single integrated design. The sinuous flow of the arm supports is counterbalanced by the related curves of the cabriole legs. The interlaced splats are serpentine in profile to avoid any area of stiffness. The artisan used the sapwood to highlight each knee and arm support in lieu of carving. The chair retains the original brown leather slip seat with the name "Brown" written on the seat in contemporary writing. This chair tripled in value in the ten years from 1962–1972 and has appreciated correspondingly since as its unsurpassed stature becomes more widely recognized.

Ht: 31½" Wd: 28¾"   Collection of Peter Eliot

ENGLISH

Queen Anne walnut corner chair, with three cabriole legs and rear turned leg, rural England, circa 1720–1750. While this English model is not meant to compete with its more sophisticated London counterparts, its understatement renders it closer to related American forms. The shapeless seat is somewhat boxy and the cabriole legs do not have the bend seen on the best colonial models.

© 1977, SOTHEBY'S, INC.

AMERICAN:
BETTER

Queen Anne walnut corner chair with four cabriole legs and cabriole arm supports, Philadelphia, circa 1740–1760. The necessarily deep apron served a contemporary function but required relatively shorter legs. This occasioned a heavy base. The heaviness is somewhat relieved by a serpentine apron, and the incurvate arm supports add stature to the form.

COURTESY OF CHRISTIE'S

AMERICAN: MASTERPIECE

Queen Anne walnut corner chair with four cabriole legs and incurvate arm supports, Philadelphia, circa 1740–1760. The height of curvilinear development in the corner chair form. The beautifully curved arm supports unite with the similarly curved cabriole legs. The curved leg and arm supports are united by a horseshoe-shaped seat, the rounded front of which blends with the contour of the knee on the frontal cabriole leg. The composition is surmounted by a yoke crest with vibrantly scrolled knuckles which brilliantly terminate the powerful movement of the undulating curves.

Ht: 30½" Wd: 28½" across arms   Metropolitan Museum of Art

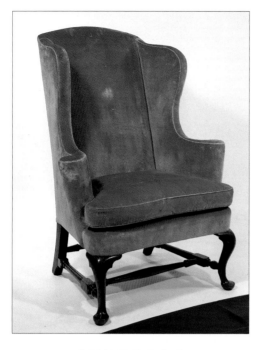

SUPERIOR

Q ueen Anne walnut upholstered wing chair, Massachusetts or Rhode Island, circa 1740–1760. A choice example of the favorite form of New England cabriole leg wing chairs. The seat frame is hewn from thick maple beams, then contoured with rounded corners to blend with the finely modeled cabriole legs and crisp wafer pad feet.

Ht: 47½" Wd: 35½"   Private collection

View of frame: This demonstrates the durability of the chair's construction, which has enabled a number of similar examples to survive intact. The cabriole legs are dovetailed into the seat frame and the back posts are one piece from the floor to the crest.

MASTERPIECE

Q ueen Anne upholstered wing chair, Townsend school, Newport, Rhode Island, circa 1740–1770. This chair vies with the Robb MASTERPIECE for stateliness and beauty of form. The flat stretchers are characteristic of a small group of chairs fashioned by the Townsends. A Newport feature is the placement of the ankle into the center of the wafer pad foot. The horizontal roll arms are more common on Philadelphia examples.

Ht: 49¾" Wd: 35½"   Private collection

MASTERPIECE

Queen Anne walnut upholstered wing chair, Rhode Island, circa 1740–1770. A gifted artisan produced this magnificent creation with an emphasis on the vertical. The beauty of this wing chair illustrates why unadorned New England Queen Anne furniture has been placed in the "art" category. The Robbs of Buffalo purchased this chair from Israel Sack in the early 1940s. We purchased it from the Robb family for ten times their cost and the value is still rising.

Ht: 48¼" Wd: 34½"   ***Private collection***

PHOTOGRAPH: ISRAEL SACK, INC.

ENGLISH

Queen Anne walnut wing chair with horizontal roll arms and cabriole front and rear legs, England, circa 1720–1730. The close similarity in form of this fine English chair with its Philadelphia masterpiece counterpart is striking, yet comparison points out the subtle differences that distinguish the Philadelphia interpretation. On this example the cabriole legs are shorter, the seat has less of a bow, and the front legs are farther to the corners.

© 1977, SOTHEBY'S, INC.

AMERICAN: BEST

Queen Anne walnut wing chair with intaglio knee carving, William Savery school, Philadelphia, circa 1740–1760. This chair does not have the fluency of the most admired Philadelphia wing chairs. It is broader and lower, with a more angular straight seat. Yet it is a fine chair showing the lamb's tongue or intaglio knee carving favored by Savery. The broad low proportion, favored more in English design, occasioned a story related by my father, Israel Sack. Henry F. du Pont purchased this chair from my father in the 1920s and had it sent to Henry Weil, a contemporary dealer. A week later Mr. du Pont called Israel Sack and said, "Mr. Sack, this chair has been questioned as English. I have great confidence in your integrity but as long as there has been a doubt expressed, do you mind if I return it?" Israel Sack replied, "Mr. du Pont, I believe that if a piece is only good for one person, it's no good. I'll accept it back with pleasure." Mr. Sack sold the chair to Mrs. Charles Hallam Keep, who exhibited it in the Girl Scout Loan Exhibition of 1929. It is now recognized as a Philadelphia chair, probably by William Savery.

Whereabouts unknown

View of frame: This shows the integrity of craftsmanship typical of the colonial upholstered chairmakers and the sculptural refinement fashioned from durable beams.

AMERICAN: MASTERPIECE

Queen Anne walnut wing chair with horizontal roll arms and cabriole front and rear legs, Philadelphia, circa 1740–1750. While cabriole rear legs are common on English wing chairs, only a few American examples exist. None are finer than this model. The greatness of this chair lies in the verticality of the chair's stance, the powerful sweep of the horizontal roll arms, the spring of the bow of the seat frame, and the form of the front cabriole legs which thrust forward toward the center in typical Philadelphia style. The overall fluidity of this chair in contrast to its English counterpart is emphasized in the comparison of the rear cabriole legs. Those of the English chair are stiff and do not have the grace or quality of integration into the back and seat frame as those on the American example.

Private collection

BETTER-BEST

Chippendale walnut claw-and-ball-foot wing chair with horizontal roll arms, Philadelphia, circa 1760–1780 (left). An important, choice example of a typical Philadelphia wing chair. It suffers only in the stiffness of the curve of the cabriole leg and the average sculpturing of the claw and ball feet as compared with the SUPERIOR example.

Whereabouts unknown
PHOTOGRAPH: JOHN HOPF

SUPERIOR

Chippendale walnut claw-and-ball-foot wing chair with horizontal roll arms, Philadelphia, circa 1760–1780 (above right and near right). This chair has always been one of my favorites, even in its understated simplicity. It stands like a thoroughbred race horse with front legs thrust forward, rear legs raking dramatically back. The narrow back and boldly bowed seat have a compact tightness.

Collection of Mrs. James Britten

Profile view.

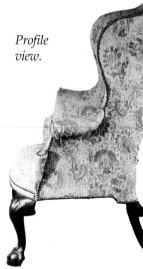

MASTERPIECE

Chippendale mahogany claw-and-ball-foot wing chair with horizontal roll arms, Philadelphia, circa 1760–1780 (left). This is a collector's dream, representing the perfection of form. It has superbly modeled acanthus-carved cabriole legs that retain their original finish. Note the bell-shaped formation of the seat frame and the outward thrust of the horizontal arms.

Private collection

GOOD

Chippendale mahogany claw-and-ball-foot wing chair, Massachusetts, circa 1760–1780 (left). A stiff angular version. The back is as stiff as a board and the armrests do not flare outward.

Whereabouts unknown

Detail of leg.

MASTERPIECE

Chippendale mahogany upholstered claw-and-ball-foot wing chair attributed to Benjamin Frothingham, Charlestown, Massachusetts, circa 1760–1780. One of the finest Chippendale wing chairs produced in Massachusetts. Note the flare of the vertical arms and the softened contours of the back. The acanthus-carved cabriole legs end in finely sculptured claw and ball feet with retracted side talons and are joined by block-and-bulbous-turned stretchers.

Ht: 46¾" Wd: 36"   Collection of Erving and Joyce Wolf
PHOTOGRAPH: ISRAEL SACK, INC.

GOOD

Sheraton mahogany upholstered wing chair with turned legs, New York, circa 1810–1820. An adequate but uninspired frame is supported on heavy, clumsy, multiple-turned legs.

COURTESY OF CHRISTIE'S

BEST

Sheraton mahogany upholstered wing chair on bulbous-turned legs, New York, circa 1800–1815. This chair exhibits pleasing lines and reasonably well-turned legs.

COURTESY OF CHRISTIE'S

MASTERPIECE

Sheraton mahogany upholstered wing chair with tapered reeded legs, Massachusetts, circa 1800–1810. Belonged to General Artemus Ward, commanding general of the Continental forces before Washington took command. To my mind this is the supreme American Sheraton wing chair. A few New York examples are its only rivals. The narrow vertical effect is accentuated by the tall tapering legs of delicacy and refinement.

Ht: 43¾" Wd: 29½"
Collection of Mr. and Mrs. Lawrence A. Fleischman

BETTER

Bow-back Windsor armchair, New England, circa 1780–1800. The bowed back, arms, and spindles lack the spring required of a top-notch Windsor. The bowl-shaped saddle seat is well modeled, except when compared to its competitor.

© 1978, SOTHEBY'S, INC.

SUPERIOR

Bow-back Windsor armchair, New England, circa 1780–1800. The back has the spring and tension of a taut bow, aided by the flair of the bulbous-turned spindles. Notice how the trimming of a little fat from the saddle seat lends a smartness to the composition. The superbly turned legs have a fine rake.

© 1977, SOTHEBY'S, INC.

Windsor comb-back brace-back side chair, New England, circa 1780–1800. This pleasing chair with nice turnings and saddle seat suffers only in comparison with the SUPERIOR and MASTERPIECE related models. The crest is undeveloped and the braces lack the extension of the other examples.

Whereabouts unknown

PHOTOGRAPHIC ARCHIVES, NATIONAL GALLERY OF ART

SUPERIOR

Windsor comb-back brace-back side chair, New England, circa 1780–1800. The excellence of this chair in comparison to the BETTER model is evident in every department. The saddle seat has finer contouring, the braces and the turned legs flare out to give vitality to the design. The cupid's bow crest rail is effective.

Whereabouts unknown

PHOTOGRAPHIC ARCHIVES, NATIONAL GALLERY OF ART

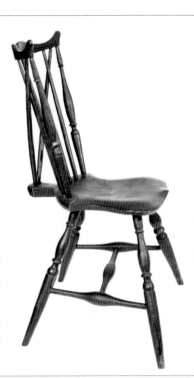

Detail: The dramatic thrust is evident in a profile view.

MASTERPIECE

Windsor fan-back brace-back side chair, New England, circa 1780–1800. A standard model transformed into a work of art by an inspired artisan. The dramatic rake to the finely turned legs is accentuated by the small contoured saddle seat and the boldly raked brace. The cupid's bow crest adds a flavor to the design. The chair retains its original paint. It is one of a pair exhibited in the 1929 Girl Scout Loan Exhibition—the mate is in the Mabel Brady Garvan Collection at Yale. This gem has passed through our hands three times, each time at a dramatic increase in value.

Ht: 34½"   Collection of Peter and Barbara Goodman

PHOTOGRAPHS: ISRAEL SACK, INC.

GOOD

Windsor comb-back writing armchair with drawer under writing tablet and seat, Connecticut, circa 1800–1810. This chair has three flaws that relegate it to a lower status despite the rarity of its form. The crest is crude, the turnings are simplistic, and the seat lacks any saddle shaping or contouring.

Whereabouts unknown

PHOTOGRAPHIC ARCHIVES, NATIONAL GALLERY OF ART

SUPERIOR

Windsor comb-back writing armchair with drawer under writing tablet and seat, attributed to Ebenezer Tracy, Lisbon, Connecticut, circa 1780–1790. Ebenezer Tracy was responsible for making a number of writing armchairs of this quality. Note the sophistication of the bulbous-turned spindles and the fine turnings and splay of the legs and arm supports. The saddle seat is scooped and shaped with finesse. This form of chair is rarely found intact with the original drawers surviving.

Ht: 45¾" Wd: 36"   Private collection

GOOD

Low-back Windsor writing armchair, **Pennsylvania, circa 1790–1810.** This chair has little to distinguish it except the writing tablet and drawer to hold writing material.

Whereabouts unknown

PHOTOGRAPHIC ARCHIVES, NATIONAL GALLERY OF ART

SUPERIOR

Low-back Windsor writing armchair, **signed Anthony Steel, Philadelphia, circa 1790–1810.** Every element of this model excels where its competitor fails. The finely turned legs support a balanced composition. The knuckle arm terminal, the ingenious double drawer under the tablet, and the drawer beneath the seat are pure refinements.

Ht: 30½" Wd: 33⅓"
Museum of Art, Rhode Island School of Design
Museum appropriation

GOOD

Comb-back Windsor armchair, Pennsylvania, circa 1780–1800 (left). A stiff, ungainly example with poor turnings.

© 1972, SOTHEBY'S, INC.

SUPERIOR

Comb-back Windsor armchair with blunt arrow turnings, Pennsylvania, circa 1770–1790 (right). A fine model with excellent blunt arrow turnings and spacious proportions. The crest has nicely scrolled ears.

Ht. 24½" Wd: 28¾" Dp: 21"
Formerly Israel Sack, Inc.
(whereabouts unknown)

MASTERPIECE

Comb-back Windsor armchair, Pennsylvania, circa 1770–1790. This chair ranks as one of the supreme examples of the Windsor chairmakers' art. It has the stance of a thoroughbred with the bold rake of its superbly turned legs supporting a tall, stately proportioned back, and finely shaped crest with scrolled ears. The knuckle arm terminals, the finely contoured saddle seat, and the original painted surface add to its stature. This is the Windsor that you hand over a blank check for and let the owner fill in the amount.

Ht: 43" Wd: 27"
Collection of Mr. and Mrs. Israel E. Liverant

BEDS

BEST

Early maple folding bed retaining the original red paint, New England, circa 1720–1760. The folding bed was the ancestor of the modern Murphy bed. Israel Sack once wrote to the Murphy bed company suggesting they use this prototype as an advertisement. The company wrote back: no chance. They wanted the public to think the idea was original to them. Not too many examples exist intact. The turnings on this bed are not as refined as the following examples.

Ht: 23" Lg: 76" Wd: 55"   Private collection

SUPERIOR

Early maple folding bed retaining the original red paint, New England, circa 1720–1760. The turnings are more refined on this example, making it more valuable.

Ht: 35" Lg: 77" Wd: 54"
Collection of Mrs. Virginia Knauer

MASTERPIECE

Early maple folding bed with original half-canopy tester frame, original red paint, New England, circa 1720–1760. One of the great rarities. Few of these tester frames have survived intact. The fine turnings of the foot posts are matched by the slender tapered pencil posts housing the headboard.

Ht: 89" Lg: 77½" Wd: 53"
Private collection

BEST

Chippendale maple Marlborough-foot bed with fluted foot posts and bulbous urn, Massachusetts, circa 1760–1780. A pleasing version of a scarce Chippendale form. Its simplicity does not take away from its appeal, especially since it has survived with the original rails and headboard.

Formerly Israel Sack, Inc.
(whereabouts unknown)

MASTERPIECE

Chippendale mahogany Marlborough-foot bed with spiral-twist urn, wheat-carved reeded posts, Goddard-Townsend, Newport, Rhode Island, circa 1760–1780. The spiral-twist urn is a feature seen on a handful of beds and some tripod tables by the master craftsmen of Newport. The plain headposts are tapered and slotted to receive the headboard. The reeded foot posts show refinement in the wheat carving and the egg-and-dart carving above the reeding.

Ht: 94½" Lg: 77" Wd: 58¾"   *Private collection*

Detail of post.

BETTER

Sheraton maple four-post bed, New Hampshire, circa 1810–1820. The turnings show a lack of finesse—evidence of a rural joiner whose specialty was not turning. The posts lack the subtle swell of the following beds. The original red paint gives it a country charm.

Ht: 76¼" Lg: 78¼" Wd: 54¼"
COURTESY OF CHRISTIE'S

SUPERIOR

Sheraton birch four-post bed, North Shore, Massachusetts, or New Hampshire, circa 1800–1815. A graceful model with beautifully turned and bulbous reeded posts. Note how the bulbous reeding tapers as it narrows to the top. This, together with the long terminal, results in a slender vertical effect.

Ht: 84½" Lg: 75¼" Wd: 53½"
Formerly Israel Sack, Inc.
(whereabouts unknown)

Detail of post.

MASTERPIECE

Sheraton mahogany four-post bed, Boston, circa 1800–1810. The ultimate in brilliant turning is combined with exceptional carved detail to result in this superb creation. The bulbous acanthus-carved urn is delicately carved with a beaded band on a cylindrical fluted plinth. The blocks receiving the rails have bird's-eye-maple veneered panels. The original rails had canvas rather than rope to hold the mattress.

Ht: 90" Lg: 77¾" Wd: 60"   Collection of Mr. and Mrs. Charles O. Smith, Jr.

BETTER

Sheraton mahogany four-post bed, Massachusetts, circa 1800–1815. The nicely reeded urn and bulbous foot posts of this bed suffer only in comparison with the SUPERIOR model. The slightly heavy turned legs have lost a few inches of height below the base turning. The bowed or serpentine tester is missing.

Ht: (top of post) 60¼" Lg: 76½" Wd: 53"
Formerly Israel Sack, Inc.
(whereabouts unknown)

SUPERIOR

Sheraton mahogany four-post tester bed, Massachusetts, circa 1800–1815. The exquisite reeded urn and bulbous foot posts of this example are rarely equaled by contemporary examples. The beautifully turned tapered legs and bulbous and tapering feet accentuate the verticality of the posts.

Ht: 88" Lg: 75½" Wd: 55¾"
Formerly Israel Sack, Inc.
(whereabouts unknown)

BETTER

Sheraton mahogany four-post bed, New York, circa 1815–1830. The somewhat heavy drapery-carved urn, combined with the long cylinder and slightly tapering acanthus-carved and reeded posts lack the delicacy and refinement of the following bed.

Whereabouts unknown

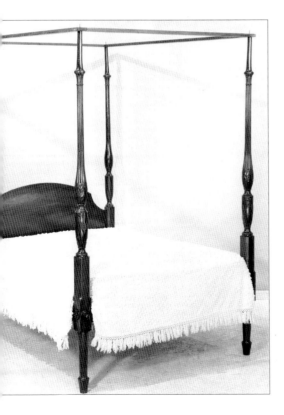

SUPERIOR

Sheraton mahogany four-post bed, Philadelphia, circa 1800–1815. The swell of the acanthus-carved and reeded posts tapers dramatically to effect a rare grace and beauty. The slender leg terminates in a round spade foot, a feature favored by the Philadelphia cabinetmaker Henry Connelly.

Ht: 94" Wd: 61"

© 1956, SOTHEBY'S, INC.

BUREAUS

BETTER

Pilgrim oak and pine one-drawer "Hadley" chest, initialed *SM*, Hadley-Northampton area of Massachusetts, circa 1690–1715. The Hadley chest is so named for a group of chests with the naïve scrolled motifs indigenous to the group. Over a hundred related chests were depicted in Luther's *The Hadley Chest* published in 1935 and they represent one of the first important groups of distinctly American design. For some reason, the carver of this chest did not complete the decoration below the three panels or on the stiles. Its absence becomes apparent upon comparison with the SUPERIOR model.

Ht: 30" Wd: 45" Dp: 20½"
The Detroit Institute of Arts
Gift of Mr. and Mrs. Edsel B. Ford

SUPERIOR

Pilgrim oak and pine one-drawer "Hadley" chest, initialed *MS*, Hadley-Northampton area of Massachusetts, circa 1690–1715. A fully developed example. Typical of the group is the stippled background for the naïve carving in old red paint which sometimes remains even when the original surface paint has been removed.

Ht: 23¼" Wd: 46¾" Dp: 19⅜"
The Brooklyn Museum, 14.707
The Henry L. Batterman Fund

MASTERPIECE

Pilgrim oak and pine three-drawer "Hadley" chest, initialed *TS*, Hadley-Northampton area of Massachusetts, circa 1690–1715. This is one of two three-drawer Hadley chests known; the other example is in Historic Deerfield. It is in a magnificent state of preservation, retaining the original red painted surface.

Ht: 51½" Wd: 45" Dp: 19"
Collection of the Dietrich Americana Foundation
PHOTOGRAPH: ISRAEL SACK, INC.

BETTER

William and Mary ball-foot bureau, American, circa 1700–1730. The rarity of authentic chests-of-drawers of this period excuses the plainness of this example. Its simplicity makes it appear earlier than the following examples, but the board construction is generally later than the frame construction of the seventeenth-century chests.

Whereabouts unknown

PHOTOGRAPHIC ARCHIVES, NATIONAL GALLERY OF ART

SUPERIOR

William and Mary walnut ball-foot bureau with geometric molded panels, Massachusetts, circa 1690–1720 (left, and detail at right). A masterful example that expresses boldness and the hand of a superior craftsman and designer. Chests-of-drawers of this period typically employ geometric panels to express creative skill. The original ball feet are attached to the base by a thick dowel which runs through the core of the foot. This bureau retains the frame construction of the seventeenth century.

Ht: 36¾" Wd: 39½" Dp: 22⅛"
Collection of E. Martin

MASTERPIECE

William and Mary oak and pine ball-foot bureau with geometric panels and original painted decoration, Massachusetts, circa 1680–1720. The incredible survival of the original paint, condition, and ball feet of this beautiful bureau makes it a priceless specimen. The center drawers have ducks within the geometric panels.

Ht: 36" Wd: 40" Dp: 19¾"
The Brooklyn Museum, 49.190.2
Bequest of Mrs. William Sterling Peters,
by exchange
PHOTOGRAPH: JUSTIN KERR

Detail: The cedar moldings and beveled frame are carefully mitered; the chased teardrop brass handles are secured by cotter pins.

SUPERIOR

Chippendale mahogany claw-and-ball-foot bureau, gadrooned apron border, New York, circa 1760–1780. The compact small-scale proportion typical in Massachusetts is not common in New York case furniture. The squared formation of the claw and ball feet is typical of New York design. The dressing slide is a rare refinement.

Formerly collection of Mr. and Mrs. Israel E. Liverant

MASTERPIECE

Chippendale mahogany claw-and-ball-foot bureau, serpentine front and sides with carved base and sliding tray, New York, circa 1760–1780. This little gem stands as one of the supreme achievements of New York case furniture. The serpentine outlines are made more dramatic by its tiny frame. The sides are hewn from solid three-inch beams. The carving is of recognizable New York design. The top measures only 16½" in depth. This bureau was one of Mitchel Taradash's early purchases from Israel Sack, Inc. We paid the heirs 150 times their cost to reacquire it.

Ht: 32" Wd: 34½" Dp: 16½"
Collection of Peter Eliot
PHOTOGRAPH: ISRAEL SACK, INC.

Detail: The gap between the rear edge of the side and the base molding is due to natural shrinkage.

BEST

Chippendale mahogany serpentine-front bureau with ogee bracket feet, Massachusetts, circa 1770–1790. A pleasing form. The ogee bracket feet have boldly spurred knee returns and the drawer fronts are veneered, yet the craftsmanship is not equal to the SUPERIOR example.

Ht: 34¼" Wd: 37½" Dp: 20"
Formerly Israel Sack, Inc.
(whereabouts unknown)

SUPERIOR

Chippendale mahogany serpentine-front bureau with ogee bracket feet, Massachusetts, circa 1760–1790. The sharp lines, superior selection of wood, and skillful craftsmanship make an exciting composition. The sweeping serpentine curve comes to a point at the edge, continuing through the ogee feet, and gives the appearance of the prow of a ship cutting through the water.

Ht: 35½" Wd: 40" Dp: 21"
Private collection

MASTERPIECE

Chippendale mahogany serpentine-front bureau with blocked ends and ogee bracket feet, Massachusetts, circa 1760–1780. A compact gem. The blocked ends serve to compress the serpentine into a bolder curve. The overhanging top is in perfect balance with the overall composition, and the golden color adds to its appeal.

Ht: 31¾" Wd: 38" Dp: 20¼"
Private collection

BETTER

Chippendale mahogany bureau with ogee bracket feet, Rhode Island, circa 1760–1780. This bureau cannot be faulted for craftsmanship, but it is broad and squarish in proportion.

Ht: 33" Wd: 41"

© 1977, SOTHEBY'S, INC.

SUPERIOR

Chippendale mahogany bureau with platformed ogee bracket feet, Philadelphia, circa 1760–1780. A finely proportioned example exhibiting craftsmanship and selection of mahogany indicative of a competent Philadelphia artisan. The fluted quarter columns soften the severity of the corners. Philadelphia bureaus do not vary in form as greatly as do their New England counterparts, so the relative stature of Philadelphia bureaus derives from different levels of quality within this standard form.

Ht: 34½" Wd: 39¼" Dp: 21¾"   ***Private collection***

MASTERPIECE

Chippendale walnut bureau with ogee bracket feet, Philadelphia, circa 1760–1780. Its compact scale of the case and superb proportion elevate this standard form to exalted status. Its composition is drawn together by the divided row of top drawers and the lively figured grain.

Ht: 33½" Wd: 32¾" Dp: 20½"   *Collection of June and Joseph Hennage*

AMERICAN: MASTERPIECE

Chippendale mahogany serpentine-front bureau with fret-carved canted corners and carved claw and ball feet, Salem, Massachusetts, circa 1780–1785. The difficulty of rigid categories is evident in the comparison of the two chefs d'oeuvre, reflecting a major achievement of Massachusetts rococo development. The carving is first rank, the craftsmanship is superb, and the claw and ball feet with swept-back talons are finely sculptured. Yet comparison with the Thomas Needham bureau is striking. This piece has a more horizontal proportion closer to the English emphasis, and the thick ankles effect a weightiness the Needham bureau overcomes.

Ht: 33⅞" Wd: 40⅞" Dp: 17⅞"
Museum of Fine Arts, Boston, M. and M. Karolik Collection

ENGLISH:
MASTERPIECE

Chippendale mahogany serpentine-front bureau with canted corners and ogee feet, England, circa 1750–1770. This bureau, of outstanding craftsmanship and carving, reflects the English emphasis on the horizontal proportion.

Whereabouts unknown

The bureau was purchased from the Cluett family in more recent times and now compares favorably in value with great American impressionist paintings, including those in the seven-figure category. The dramatic sequence to this saga is recounted in American Treasure Hunt: The Legacy of Israel Sack *by Harold Sack with Max Wilk (Little, Brown & Co., 1986, pp. 99–108).*

AMERICAN: MASTERPIECE

Chippendale mahogany serpentine-front bureau with fret-carved canted corners (carved from the solid) and carved claw and ball feet, made by Thomas Needham, Jr., Salem, Massachusetts, signed *"TN 1783."* We consider this the supreme bureau fashioned in Massachusetts in the Colonial era. It is the same basic form as the Karolik bureau but has a power and majesty all its own. The proportions show how a genius can transform various masterpiece elements into a masterpiece composition. The lift and tensile strength of the ankles and the relative narrowness and height of the case creates a verticality and superb proportion. Israel Sack recognized this masterpiece early in his career. His record of ownership, in his handwriting, traces the remarkable rise in value of American antiques in this century.

Ht: 36½" Wd: 44¼" Dp: 24¼"
Private collection
PHOTOGRAPHS: ISRAEL SACK, INC.

Detail: This profile view shows the powerful serpentine sweep framed by the canted fretwork columns.

BETTER

Chippendale walnut serpentine-front bureau with canted corners, Philadelphia or vicinity, circa 1760–1780. While the general form relates to the following MASTERPIECE, this bureau lacks the refinement of the latter. This is apparent in the lack of beaded drawer borders and the blandness of the wood patterns. The small size is attractive and unusual for this form.

Ht: 34" Wd: 30½" Dp: 23"
Whereabouts unknown

Detail of top.

MASTERPIECE

Chippendale mahogany serpentine-front bureau with canted corners and ogee feet, **Philadelphia, circa 1760–1780.** The powerful sweeping curves, enhanced by the figured grain and the broad chamfered ogee feet and columns, all make the large scale of this piece necessary. The bold ogee feet are skillfully modeled to avoid heaviness, the front and side façades follow the incurvate outline of the case, and the inner outline of the feet have a sharply defined contouring. The rich crotch figure of the top (see detail, opposite) becomes even more remarkable when it is realized that the top is hewn from a solid board.

Ht: 39" Wd: 46½" Dp: 26"   Private collection

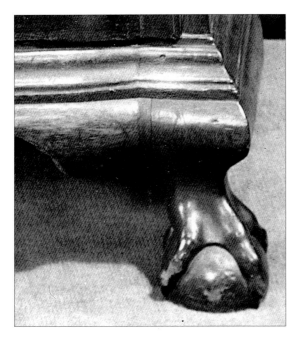

Detail of foot.

BETTER

Chippendale mahogany oxbow bureau with claw and ball feet, **Massachusetts, circa 1760–1780.** This bureau has many desirable features: compact size, blocked ends, and bold brasses. The claw and ball feet are flaccid and the talons lack authority.

Whereabouts unknown

MASTERPIECE

Chippendale mahogany oxbow bureau with claw and ball feet, Salem, Massachusetts, circa 1760–1780 (one of a rare pair of matched bureaus). This compact gem displays a bolder serpentine outline enhanced by superbly figured grain and deeply defined blocked ends. The claw and ball feet are finely sculptured (see detail) and the overhang of the top is in perfect balance.

Ht: 32½" Wd: 36¾" Dp: 21¼"
Private collection

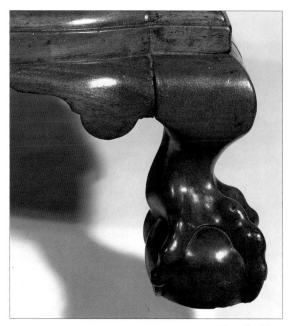

Detail of foot.

BETTER

Chippendale cherry oxbow bureau with blocked ends, Massachusetts, circa 1760–1780. The main weakness of this otherwise desirable bureau is the close-cropped top, which does not hold the piece's composition together. The blocked ends do not achieve the effect of boldness that the following examples attain.

Whereabouts unknown

SUPERIOR

Chippendale mahogany oxbow bureau with blocked ends, attributed to Benjamin Frothingham, Charlestown, Massachusetts, circa 1760–1780. A dynamic example: the compact case exudes power and is enhanced by choice flaming grain mahogany. The double-ogee feet are also seen on a chest-on-chest labeled *Benjamin Frothingham.*

Ht: 30½" Wd: 38" Dp: 20½"
Collection of Norton N. Katz

MASTERPIECE

Pair of Chippendale mahogany oxbow bureaus with blocked ends, authenticated to John Chipman, Salem, Massachusetts, circa 1760–1785. Each of these bureaus can be considered a masterpiece; as a pair they have no equals. They excel in proportion, magnificent solid figured grain, and superior craftsmanship. The exciting flourish of the spurred and cyma-scrolled base outline and the distinctive central pendant are the main basis for authentication to John Chipman. (See the magazine *Antiques*, December 1987, for definitive article on Chipman by Donald Sack and Peter Louis.)

Ht: 35" Wd: 39" Dp: 23½"   *Diplomatic Reception Rooms, United States Department of State*

BETTER

Chippendale mahogany block-front bureau, Massachusetts, circa 1760–1780. It is difficult to find a less than high-quality block-front bureau, as this form was generally fashioned only by competent craftsmen. Compared to the following bureaus, the blocking on this example is less bold and does not have the impact of its competitors.

Whereabouts unknown

SUPERIOR

Chippendale mahogany block-front bureau, Massachusetts, circa 1760–1780. It is evident that this is the work of a master craftsman of the caliber of Benjamin Frothingham or John Cogswell. The boldness of the blocking is accentuated by the choice figured grain and the equally bold willow brasses. It should be realized that the blocking on this and most block-front case pieces is hewn from a solid piece.

Private collection

MASTERPIECE
examples appear on
pages 106 and 107.

MASTERPIECE

Unique Queen Anne mahogany small block-front bureau with ten drawers, Massachusetts, circa 1740–1755. A creative innovator divided each of the three lower drawers into a row of three drawers without sacrificing the unity of the composition. The extended view shows the ingenuity and practicality of this conception. The early influence of the piece is evidenced by the original bat wing brasses and broad cyma-shaped brackets. The bureau's stature is enhanced by a mellow brown patina of great depth.

Ht: 30½" Wd: 33¾" Dp: 20¾"
Private collection

Detail of drawers extended.

SUPERIOR

Chippendale mahogany block-front bureau, Massachusetts, circa 1750–1770. This block-front bureau form is native to the colonies. The largest number were produced in Massachusetts, and they are of uniformly high quality, as is this one. Its beauty is enhanced by a warm, mellow patina. The original bat wing brasses suggest the Queen Anne influence.

Ht: 30½" Wd: 35½" Dp: 20¼"
Private collection

MASTERPIECE

Chippendale mahogany block-front bureau with dressing slide, Massachusetts, circa 1760–1780. The bureau's dynamic proportions and its compact case with dramatic overhang transform this creation into a masterwork. The piece is fashioned from dense San Domingan mahogany and the bold blocking with original large willow brasses serves to create a vertical emphasis. The dressing slide is a rare feature.

Ht: 32⅛" Wd: 34½" Dp: 21¼"   *Collection of Mr. and Mrs. Robert Lee Gill*
PHOTOGRAPH: ISRAEL SACK, INC.

SUPERIOR

Chippendale mahogany bombe bureau with serpentine front, carved knees, and carved claw and ball feet, Massachusetts, circa 1760–1780. The small group of bombe pieces with serpentine fronts is the ultimate achievement of the bombe form. The purpose of the design is to overcome the mass of the piece. It is a tour de force of cabinetmaking skill, considering the complexity of fashioning all elements from the solid. Yet this example does not fully succeed in eliminating a heavy effect. The bombe section swells abruptly, and the relative proportion does not accentuate a vertical emphasis. The carving is first rank, but the ankles are thick, adding to the heavy effect. This is rather harsh criticism of a great American achievement, but it is useful to prove our contention that successful form, proportion, and verticality are the paramount yardsticks in grading American designs.

Ht: 33½" Wd: 33⅞" Dp: 18¾"
Museum of Fine Arts, Boston, M. and M. Karolik Collection

MASTERPIECE

Chippendale mahogany bombe bureau with serpentine front and claw and ball feet, Boston, circa 1775–1790 (right). This magnificent gem ranks high on the list of supreme achievements of the Boston master craftsmen. It delights the eye in every aspect: the compact case, the smooth swell of the serpentine sides, the superb figured mahogany grain which sweeps along the sides and top like a flaming sunset, the rococo Chinese Chippendale brasses, the golden patina, and the integration of the claw and ball feet with the case. The petite case and the fine gilded brasses suggest a post-Revolutionary date.

Ht: 31½" Wd: 35¾" Dp: 20¼"   Collection of the Dietrich Americana Foundation
PHOTOGRAPH: ISRAEL SACK, INC.

Detail of side.

Detail of brass.

BETTER

Chippendale mahogany block-front bureau with claw and ball feet, Massachusetts, circa 1760–1780. The legs seem too tall and angular for the compact case. Together with the exaggerated overhang, the design does not achieve the integration of the comparative MASTERPIECE.

Ht: 32½" Wd: 38¾"

© 1976, SOTHEBY'S, INC.

BETTER

Chippendale mahogany block-front bureau with claw and ball feet, Massachusetts, circa 1760–1780. This bureau is of high quality, but it is slightly boxy in proportion due to the ratio of height to width.

Whereabouts unknown

MASTERPIECE

Chippendale mahogany block-front bureau with claw and ball feet, Massachusetts, circa 1760–1780. The bold character of this fine bureau is achieved with perfect integration of its component parts. The outer edge of the blocking continues onto the cabriole of the foot, and the rounded blocking continues in unbroken line onto the knee bracket, allowing for a smooth transition of the two elements. Its beauty is aided by the superb color and excellent original condition.

Ht: 33¼" Wd: 38" Dp: 21¾"
Collection of June and Joseph Hennage

SUPERIOR

Chippendale mahogany block-and-shell-carved bureau, Goddard-Townsend, Newport, Rhode Island, circa 1760–1780. Any block-and-shell piece produced by one of the Goddards or Townsends is of the utmost importance. This chest-of-drawers evidences the handiwork of one of these master craftsmen. A minor criticism lies in the drawer ratio. By emphasizing the depth of the shell-carved drawer, the maker had to compress the three lower drawers into a smaller area.

Ht: 32½" Wd: 36⅛" Dp: 20"

© 1988, SOTHEBY'S, INC.

MASTERPIECE

Chippendale mahogany block-and-shell-carved bureau, labeled *John Townsend*, Newport, Rhode Island, made in 1790. No Newport cabinetmaker made finer shells than John Townsend, and few pieces by other makers of the Goddard and Townsend families equal his. The proportions of this piece are more satisfying due to the proper drawer ratio. The superb original condition and finish add to its stature.

Ht: 34½" Wd: 36¼" Dp: 19¼"
The Serri Collection

BETTER

Chippendale mahogany bombe bureau with claw and ball feet, Massachusetts, circa 1760–1780. The bombe bureau form is known to have been produced only in Massachusetts and any example of the few extant is important. The success of the form depends on the proportion and the subtlety of the serpentine curve of the sides. Compared to the following masterpiece, this example has too much breadth, and the transition line is not as smooth at the beginning of the curve. The knee brackets are not as integrated to the case as they are in the MASTERPIECE.

Ht: 32½" Wd: 40" Dp: 20¼"
Whereabouts unknown
PHOTOGRAPH: ISRAEL SACK, INC.

MASTERPIECE

Chippendale mahogany bombe bureau with claw and ball feet, Salem, Massachusetts, circa 1760–1780. The case is more compact, reducing a feeling of mass. The base is superbly integrated with the case. The cyma-curved and lobed knee brackets and winged center convex shell pendant form a pattern all their own.

Ht: 35¼" Dp: 22¼" Wd: 40"   *Courtesy Henry Francis du Pont Winterthur Museum*

BETTER

Hepplewhite cherry serpentine-front bureau, Massachusetts, circa 1780–1810. An otherwise pleasing form is downgraded because of bracket feet that lack a definite outline and a top with plain, blunt edges.

Whereabouts unknown

SUPERIOR

Hepplewhite mahogany inlaid serpentine-front bureau, Norfolk, Virginia, circa 1780–1810. A study in grace and fine proportion. The outsplayed French feet complete the fine ogival-curved line of the apron.

Ht: 39⅛" Wd: 43¾" Dp: 23½"
Collection of the Museum of Early Southern Decorative Arts, #2033.37

MASTERPIECE

Hepplewhite mahogany serpentine-front bureau, with veneered figured birch three-paneled front and drop panel, Portsmouth, New Hampshire, circa 1780–1810. The exciting and carefully matched figured grain contained in cross-banded borders is seen on several fine bow-front bureaus but rarely on a serpentine-front example. The richness of the figured grain is matched by the brilliance of the bureau's stately form.

Ht: 30" Wd: 40½" Dp: 21½"
Metropolitan Museum of Art,
gift of Mrs. Russell Sage, 1909

BETTER

Sheraton mahogany bow-front bureau with turret columns and carved capitals, Salem, Massachusetts, circa 1815–1830. The carefully chosen grain and refinement of the reeded top edge is marred by slightly heavy reeded columns and legs. The carving is adequate but does not compare with the carved capitals of the SUPERIOR example.

Ht: 41" Wd: 45½" Dp: 23½"
Whereabouts unknown

SUPERIOR

Sheraton mahogany bow-front bureau with turret columns and carved capitals, attributed to William Hook, Salem, Massachusetts, circa 1800–1815. A master craftsman collaborated with a master carver, possibly Samuel McIntire, to fashion an elegant creation from the large, commodious model. The finely turned legs, the ringed top edge, the choice mottled mahogany veneer, and the acanthus-carved capitals with star-punch, or snowflake, background contribute to its excellence.

Ht: 42" Wd: 43¼" Dp: 22"
Private collection

CHESTS-ON-CHESTS

BETTER

Chippendale cherry bonnet-top chest-on-chest with fan-carved center drawer, Connecticut, circa 1770–1790 (right). A better than average chest with a nicely carved fan drawer and spiral quarter-columns. The arch does not have enough lift and the bracket feet are underdeveloped.

Ht: 85" Wd: 38" Dp: 18½"
Whereabouts unknown

SUPERIOR

Chippendale cherry bonnet-top chest-on-chest with fan-carved center drawer, Salem, Massachusetts, or vicinity, circa 1770–1790 (left). A dynamic small-scale chest-on-chest by a superior artisan. The proportions are exemplary. The fluted columns support a beautifully shaped arch. The spurred center plinth and individualistic flame finials add a flair to the competent design. The deeply carved fan and the ogee bracket feet show the hand of a first-class craftsman.

Ht: 86" Wd: 39¼" Dp: 21"
Private collection

BETTER

Chippendale cherry bonnet-top block-front chest-on-chest, Massachusetts, circa 1760–1780. Most block-front Massachusetts chests-on-chests were of such high quality it is hard to find one to criticize. This one is also in *Fine Points I.* It is somewhat boxy in proportion. The bonnet opening is cramped and the fluted quarter-columns are not as effective as the flat fluted pilasters in the MASTERPIECE example.

Whereabouts unknown

MASTERPIECE

Chippendale mahogany bonnet-top block-front chest-on-chest, Massachusetts, circa 1760–1780. The gradation in width of the upper case results in a pyramidal effect which the BETTER example lacks. The proportions are exemplary and emphasize a vertical thrust aided by the high-arch bonnet. The fluted pilasters effectively reduce the breadth of the drawers, and the shaped top-end drawers follow the line of the arch. The beauty is aided by a golden patina and carved open flame finials.

Ht: 90" Wd: 42½" Dp: 22½"
Private collection

SUPERIOR

Chippendale walnut scroll-top chest-on-chest with shell-and-vine-carved center drawer, Philadelphia, circa 1760–1780 (descended in the Morris family) (right). The slender proportion, the beautiful high rise of the arch and the ample arch opening accomplish the strong vertical proportion. Note the three-and two-drawer arrangement of the two upper rows of drawers, which serves to tighten the composition. The original finish and condition add to the stature of this fine chest and make it worth several times its comparative BETTER example.

Ht: 93½" Wd: 42½" Dp: 22½"
Private collection

BETTER

Chippendale mahogany scroll-top chest-on-chest with shell-and-vine-carved center drawer, Philadelphia, circa 1760–1780 (left). The only criticism of this fine Philadelphia chest-on-chest is the flatness of the arch, which effects a squareness to the design.

Whereabouts unknown

Detail of carved phoenix ornament.

MASTERPIECE

Chippendale San Domingan mahogany scroll-top chest-on-chest with carved phoenix ornament, made by Thomas Affleck for William Logan, Philadelphia, circa 1770–1780. A magnificent creation supporting an equally magnificent carved phoenix ornament. The narrow proportion offers a verticality rare in Philadelphia case pieces. The fronts are fashioned from solid crotch-figured mahogany, and the chased bail brasses are original.

Ht: 97½" Wd: 45⅛" Dp: 22⅞"
Metropolitan Museum of Art
PHOTOGRAPH: ISRAEL SACK, INC.

BETTER

Chippendale cherry scroll-top chest-on-chest, Connecticut, circa 1770–1790. This chest has a number of good features, such as the important scroll top and the carved fans, but it falls short in comparison to the finer examples. The arch is too stiff, the feet are rather heavy, and the base would have been more successful with four drawers.

Ht: 81½" Wd: 38" Dp: 18½"
Whereabouts unknown

BETTER

Chippendale cherry scroll-top chest-on-chest, Connecticut, circa 1770–1790. The use of fluted quarter-columns does not prevent this case from being broad and rather boxy. The scroll top with dentil molding, its bold plinth shell and carved arch terminals (formerly called swastikas), is exceptional, even though the arch rises slightly abruptly.

Formerly Israel Sack, Inc.
(whereabouts unknown)

SUPERIOR

Chippendale cherry scroll-top chest-on-chest, Connecticut, circa 1770–1790. The innovative carvings of pinwheels, fans, and freestanding spiral columns are blended into a highly successful composition. The beauty of this piece is enhanced both by its excellent proportion and the exceptional old surface quality.

Ht: 82" Wd: 41¼" Dp: 21¼"
The Connecticut Historical Society, 1959-8-1,
Gift of Frederick K. and Margaret R. Barbour
PHOTOGRAPH: ISRAEL SACK, INC.

MASTERPIECE

Chippendale cherry scroll-top block-and-shell-carved chest-on-chest, Connecticut, circa 1770–1790. This magnificent piece brings the power and imagination of the fiercely independent Connecticut craftsman to its greatest height. Though the shells, the carved rosettes, and the finials are derived from more conventional centers, the cabinetmaker felt compelled to form his own creative variations. With all its boldness and drama, it is well contained and balanced.

Mr. and Mrs. Jerome Blum

MASTERPIECE: RURAL

Chippendale cherry oxbow-front scroll-top chest-on-chest, attributed to Eliphalet Chapin, East Windsor, Connecticut, circa 1770–1790 (below). Connecticut Valley craftsmen were located away from the coastal centers and were therefore less sophisticated and less academically trained than those from the larger centers. They were fiercely independent, and though they adopted forms and motifs from other centers, they used these variations in a creative manner. In this case, the chest's basic form is derived from the Philadelphia school, as is evident in the fluted quarter-columns, the ogee bracket feet, and the carved scrolled arch terminals. A Massachusetts influence is seen in the relationship to the oxbow drawer of the comparative Massachusetts urban example. The intertwining vines is a favorite motif of the Chapins. The proportion and integration of this piece are exemplary and the design is highly creative.

Ht: 89⅛" Wd: 45⅛" Dp: 21½"
Israel Sack, Inc.

MASTERPIECE: URBAN

Chippendale mahogany oxbow-front scroll-top chest-on-chest, attributed to Benjamin Frothingham, Charlestown, Massachusetts, circa 1770–1780 (below). Master craftsmen of the caliber of Benjamin Frothingham had more academic training than rural craftsmen and the resulting refinement is apparent here. The oxbow drawer has a more delineated outline, and the double-ogee bracket feet continue the line of the serpentine curve. The fluted corinthian columns, the finely carved capitals, the fan-carved drawer, carved terminals, and flame finials are skillfully modeled. The original patina and bold brasses add to the piece's impact.

Ht: 88½" Wd: 42"
Formerly Israel Sack, Inc. (private collection)

BETTER

Chippendale mahogany block-front scroll-top chest-on-chest with rococo-carved shell center drawer; school of Benjamin Frothingham, Boston or Charlestown, Massachusetts, circa 1760–1780. The weakness of the form is the flattened arch, which pushes down on the case. The chamfered fluted corners do not frame the upper case as effectively as the fluted columns on its counterpart.

Whereabouts unknown

PHOTOGRAPHIC ARCHIVES, NATIONAL GALLERY OF ART

MASTERPIECE

Chippendale mahogany block-front scroll-top chest-on-chest with rococo-carved shell center drawer, attributed to Benjamin Frothingham, Charlestown, Massachusetts, circa 1760–1780. This piece excels not only in the choice carving of the center drawer and open flame finials, but also in the beauty of its slender proportion. Note how the high arch of the bonnet adds to its verticality.

Ht: 91½" Wd: 41¾" Dp: 21½"
Private collection

BETTER

Chippendale maple bonnet-top chest-on-chest, Connecticut, circa 1770–1790 (left). Though the proportions of this chest-on-chest are pleasing, the simplicity of the plain scrollboard and the naïve center plinth result in a lack of integration between the crest and upper case.

Ht: 98½" Wd: 38½" Dp: 19"
© 1988, SOTHEBY'S, INC.

BEST

Chippendale cherry scroll-top chest-on-chest, Connecticut, circa 1770–1790 (right). This chest-on-chest has nice narrow proportions aided by fluted quarter-columns. A fine fan-carved row of drawers and dentil molding give a tightness to the design that is not matched by the plain scrollboard.

Ht: 87" Wd: 38½" Dp: 19½"
Private collection

SUPERIOR

Chippendale cherry scroll-top chest-on-chest, Connecticut, circa 1770–1790. A well-integrated composition. The scrolled arch outline with dentil frieze molding forms a better frame than in the BEST example. There is an obvious relationship between this example and the more developed MASTERPIECE.

Ht: 88" Wd: 40" Dp: 19½"
© 1988, SOTHEBY'S, INC.

Detail of bonnet top with drawer.

MASTERPIECE

Chippendale cherry scroll-top chest-on-chest, Connecticut, circa 1770–1790. The spirit of an independent designer of creative genius transformed this basic form into a masterpiece. The exotically carved palmetto leaves on the scrollboard front a bonnet drawer contained in a competent arch with tubular-shaped finials. The base, supported on bandy legs with pad feet, has a gadrooned molding, cyma-shaped brackets, and a broad center pendant that integrate well with the case. The old finish of the chest adds to its appeal.

Ht: 92″ Wd: 41¾″ Dp: 19¼″
Private collection
PHOTOGRAPH: ISRAEL SACK, INC.

Here are two MASTERPIECES that combine the highest expressions of the art of the cabinetmaker with the art of the carver. Each craftsman adopts the same basic format of a Classical tour de force using a Chippendale case as his instrument. Each reaches exalted heights in design, yet each develops a dramatically different character.

MASTERPIECE

Classical mahogany chest-on-chest, made by Stephen Badlam of Dorchester, Massachusetts, carving by Simeon Skillin, Boston, made for Elias Hasket Derby as a wedding present for his daughter in 1791. While Classical and post-Revolutionary influence are apparent in the design in both this chest and in the Lemon chest, the Chippendale character dominates more in this example. This massive piece expresses power and masculinity. Compared with the Lemon chest, this has a much broader proportion, and the carving by Skillin is more free hand. Though the carving on the Lemon piece is technically perfect, this carving has a vitality and spirit all its own.

Ht: 101½" Wd: 51½" Dp: 23⅜"
Courtesy Yale University Art Gallery
Mabel Brady Garvan Collection

MASTERPIECE

Classical mahogany chest-on-chest, made by William Lemon and carved by Samuel McIntire for Elias Hasket Derby, Salem, Massachusetts, 1796. One can hardly challenge the observation that this McIntire chest-on-chest is supreme. Many students of American furniture agree that if one piece were to be chosen to represent American Colonial achievement, this McIntire chest-on-chest would be a leading contender. McIntire's carving is perfect and precise. Each star in the background is clearly punched; the acanthus and other carvings are sharp, ridged, and technically perfect. The Classical lady ornament, the familiar basket, the superb urn ornaments, and the putti show the supreme handiwork of a master carver rather than a sculptor. The craftsman William Lemon was equal to the genius of his associate. He contained the elements in a superbly proportioned and integrated composition. The richly figured mahogany drawer fronts with checkered inlaid borders serve to draw the elements together.

Ht: 102½" Wd: 46¾" Dp: 23"
Courtesy Museum of Fine Arts, Boston
M. and M. Karolik Collection

SUPERIOR

Chippendale maple claw-and-ball-foot chest-on-chest, New Hampshire, circa 1780 (below). The narrow proportion and verticality of this chest are accentuated by the grain of the curly maple drawer fronts. The use of dentil molding, the repeat of graceful fans in the upper and lower sections, the center pendant drop, and tall, well-carved claw and ball feet are added refinements attesting to the ability of an accomplished non-urban cabinetmaker.

Collection of Mr. and Mrs. Andrew Lin

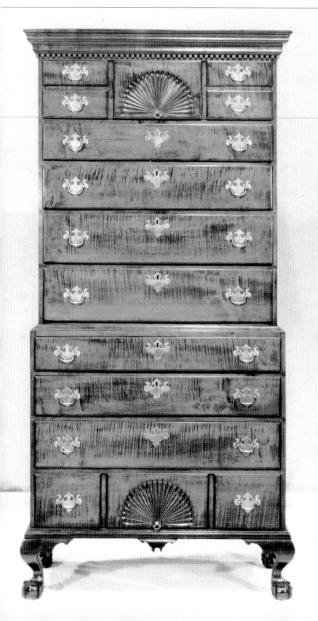

BEST

Chippendale mahogany claw-and-ball-foot chest-on-chest, New York, circa 1760–1780 (above). Attributed to Thomas Burling, this chest with chamfered and fluted corners has a fine cornice and strong claw and ball feet. The wide proportion is typical of New York case pieces, tending to give a more horizontal feeling than the SUPERIOR and MASTERPIECE examples. The craftsmanship rivals that of other main Colonial centers.

Ht: 79½" Wd: 48" Dp: 22½"
Collection of Mrs. Norman Bley

BETTER

Queen Anne maple chest-on-chest-on-frame, New Hampshire, circa 1770–1800 (right). This basically plain chest-on-chest is supported by a frame, with heavy and relatively crude cabriole legs and a similarly coarse apron.

Whereabouts unknown

SUPERIOR

Queen Anne maple chest-on-chest-on-frame, John Dunlap school. New Hampshire, circa 1770–1800 (left). A choice example with exquisitely slender, graceful cabriole legs that add lift to the design. The lively apron, with the salamander scrolls and sunburst carvings, is typical of the Dunlap family of craftsmen. The top row of three divided drawers breaks the monotony of plain surfaces. The old or original surface adds to the appeal.

Ht: 77" Wd: 40" Dp: 18½"
Israel Sack, Inc.

MASTERPIECE

Queen Anne curly maple chest-on-chest-on-frame, attributed to John Dunlap, New Hampshire, circa 1770–1800. This piece, probably the supreme Dunlap creation, can only be described in superlatives. In spite of its naïveté and exotic exuberance, it is a balanced, well-integrated composition. The widely overhanging crest, with its fans, shells, scrolls, and palmetto leaves integrates dramatically with the narrow case with complex egg-and-dart moldings. All is balanced by an equally bold and complex base. Consider the genius of a rural cabinetmaker making a creation as complex as this, which nevertheless holds together so brilliantly that the eye can only observe the whole composition as a single entity.

Ht: 82⅝" Wd: 36" Dp: 16⅞"
Currier Gallery of Art, Manchester, New Hampshire
PHOTOGRAPH: ISRAEL SACK, INC.

BETTER

Painted glass-door cupboard, Pennsylvania, circa 1800–1820. The most that can be said for this cupboard, a favorite Pennsylvania German form, is that it serves a useful storage function.

Ht: 71½" Wd: 49¼"

© 1978, SOTHEBY'S, INC.

MASTERPIECE

Painted and decorated glass-door cupboard, Reading, Pennsylvania, area, circa 1800–1820. An inspired artisan transformed this utilitarian cupboard into an art form. He created a design in the upper sections with his arrangement of the glass doors and central compartment, crowned by a boldly overhanging cornice. The base has a row of three drawers and fielded paneled doors. The original tan and green decoration gives it great appeal.

Ht: 83½" Wd: 73" Dp: 18"
The Museum of Fine Arts, Houston,
The Bayou Bend Collection
Gift of Miss Ima Hogg

CLOCKS

GOOD

Chippendale walnut tall-case clock
with broken-arch pediment, Pennsylvania, circa 1780–1800 (right). While
the general proportions of this clock are
satisfactory, the waist door is too narrow, leaving blank areas between the
quarter-columns. The pediment has a
cramped arch opening, leaving a broad
expanse of plain scrollboard.

Ht: 94½" Wd: 19"

© 1988, SOTHEBY'S, INC.

SUPERIOR

Chippendale walnut tall-case clock
with broken-arch pediment, made
by Frederick Heisley, Frederick, Maryland, circa 1780–1800 (left). The proportions of this case are very satisfying. The
base panel and waist door integrate well
into the design, and the hood has a proper arch opening.

Ht: 99¾" Wd: 18½" Dp: 9½"
Private collection

MASTERPIECE

Chippendale mahogany tall-case clock with broken arch pediment and carved scrollboard, made by John Wood, Philadelphia, circa 1760–1780. One of the supreme Philadelphia clocks, it excels in proportion, particularly in the integration of the hood with the waist. Often the hood overpowers a narrow waist, as in the GOOD example. The recessed base panel with serpentine molded borders is effective. The quality of the case combined with the beautiful carving on the scrollboard suggests the joint efforts of a master cabinetmaker, carver, and clockmaker working in harmony.

Ht: 103" Wd: 18¾" Dp: 9"
The Art Institute of Chicago, The Helen Bower Blair Fund
PHOTOGRAPH: ISRAEL SACK, INC.

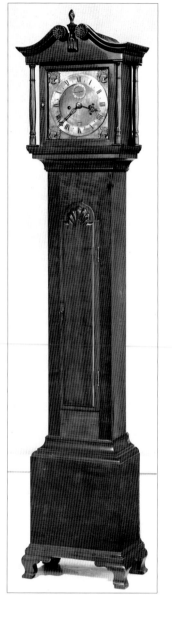

GOOD

Chippendale cherry block-and-shell-carved tall-case clock. Rhode Island or Connecticut, circa 1770–1780 (near left). This clock shows the handiwork of a lesser craftsman familiar with Newport productions but lacking the skill of the masters. The slender waist is out of proportion to the hood and base. The shell carving is crude and the arch is flat. The door is too small even for the narrow waist.

Whereabouts unknown

BETTER

Chippendale mahogany block-and-shell-carved tall-case clock, Newport, Rhode Island, circa 1770–1790 (far left). A desirable case of an important form, yet it does not reach the heights of its MASTERPIECE relative. The carved shell is slightly more refined than the GOOD example, but cannot compare to the following. The blocked door and base panels leave too much blank area as background.

© SOTHEBY'S, INC.

MASTERPIECE

Chippendale San Domingan mahogany block-and-shell-carved tall-case clock attributed to John Townsend, Newport, Rhode Island, circa 1760–1770. The mastery of form, proportion, and skillfully placed detail by one of the Goddard-Townsend group is evident here. The superbly carved shell (see detail) and boldly blocked door adequately fill the waist, which is flanked by stop-fluted quarter-columns. The base panel has chamfered corners which effectively soften the edges.

Ht: 98" Wd: 19½" Dp: 10"
Private collection
PHOTOGRAPH: ISRAEL SACK, INC.

Detail of shell.

GOOD

Hepplewhite maple tall-case clock with scrolled cresting, Riley Whiting, Winchester, Connecticut, circa 1810–1820. While this clock is half a century younger than the Harland clock and is relatively crude, it shows the influence of the earlier design. The base panel and waist door are severely plain, and the scrolled cresting should never have left Winchester.

Ht: 91"

© 1972, SOTHEBY'S, INC.

SUPERIOR

Chippendale mahogany tall-case clock with scrolled cresting, silver-engraved dial by Thomas Harland, Norwich, Connecticut, circa 1760–1780. Thomas Harland was Connecticut's most notable silversmith as well as clockmaker. His beautifully engraved, silvered dial is contained in a competent, simple case made more interesting by its scalloped base border, scrolled ogee bracket feet, spurred and voluted cresting, and lively, attenuated flame finials.

Ht: 90" Wd: 18½"
Formerly Israel Sack, Inc.
(whereabouts unknown)

Detail of base.

Detail of face.

MASTERPIECE

Chippendale cherry tall-case clock with block-and-shell-carved door and base, with ivory reeds and capitals, dial by Thomas Harland, case by Abishai Woodward, Norwich, Connecticut, circa 1775–1795. Thomas Harland's supreme achievement is breathtaking in its magnificence and competence. The incredible fact is that with all the dramatic elements— the shells, the ivory ornament, the spiral columns, the exotic base apron—the case is an integrated unit with no dominating or superfluous element. The blocking is bold and authoritative, the shell carvings compare with the best work of John Townsend, and the influence of Newport is apparent in the shell carving and rosette-arch capitals. The mastery of the case is matched by the beauty of the engraved dial.

Ht: 87½"
The Detroit Institute of Arts, gift of Mrs. Alger Shelden, Mrs. Susan Kjellberg, Mrs. Lyman Wite, Alexander Muir Duffield, and Mrs. Oliver Pendar, in memory of Helen Pitts Parker

BETTER

Hepplewhite pine tall clock, Samuel Ranlet in Monmouth District, Maine, circa 1815–1825 (right). A rural clock but with some high-style features of the Willard school such as the quarter-columns and the fretwork. The waist is relatively wide. The plain board waist door and base lack the refinement of the finer examples.

Ht: 88½" Wd: 18"
COURTESY OF CHRISTIE'S

SUPERIOR

Hepplewhite mahogany inlaid tall clock, Josiah Wood, New Bedford, Massachusetts, circa 1790–1810 (below right). A finely proportioned example with well-placed inlay. The figured mahogany grain, the fan inlaid quadrants, the molded door frame, and the stop-fluted quarter-columns with brass reeds all reflect the design and quality of the Willard school of clockmaking.

Ht: 94" Wd: 18" Dp: 9"
Dr. and Mrs. Clifford A. Poppens

MASTERPIECE

Hepplewhite mahogany inlaid tall clock, made by Simon Willard for Micah Burne, Roxbury, Massachusetts, circa 1790–1810 (left). The beauty of this choice presentation clock by New England's premier clockmaker is taken to another dimension by the dynamic proportions and rare small size. The enameled dial with rocking ship bears the inscription: *Warranted* [sic] *for Mr. Micah Burne—Simon Willard.* The label inside the door was engraved by Isaiah Thomas, Worcester, Massachusetts.

Ht: 86" Wd: 19" Dp: 9½"
Private collection

MASTERPIECE

Hepplewhite mahogany inlaid tall clock, case made in the workshop of Luther Metcalf, Medway, Massachusetts, possibly by an apprentice, Ichabod Sanford in 1796; the works made by Caleb Wheaton, Providence, Rhode Island. This superb example rivals, or surpasses, the best of the Willard creations. The rich inlays are so skillfully handled they enhance, though do not overpower, the design. The fretwork frieze in the arched hood appears on a small number of Willard cases. The interesting fact is that but for this magnificent clock, Luther Metcalf would be only known as an obscure local cabinetmaker.

Ht: 96" Wd: 19½"   *Private collection*

© 1991, SOTHEBY'S, INC.

GOOD

Hepplewhite cherry scroll-top tall clock, New York or New Jersey, circa 1800–1815 (left). The case is severely plain but has nice French feet, apron, and scrolled arch. The waist is broad with little to relieve the plain surface.

Whereabouts unknown

BETTER-BEST

Hepplewhite mahogany inlaid tall clock, New York or New Jersey, circa 1790–1810 (right). The refinement of this case is evident when compared to the GOOD example. The arched and crossbanded waist door is flanked by fluted quarter-columns supported on plinths that soften the squareness of the case and add to the vertical effect. The arch has a fine swan neck curve, but the scrollboard is relatively plain. Also, the waist door rests on the coved base molding and lacks the lift of the SUPERIOR model. The small size adds to the clock's desirability.

Ht: 85" Wd: 17½" Dp: 10"
Formerly Israel Sack, Inc.
(whereabouts unknown)

SUPERIOR

Hepplewhite mahogany inlaid tall clock, case labeled by John Scudder, Westfield, New Jersey, circa 1800–1815 (left). A beautifully proportioned case with a finely scrolled apron and a high-perched, graceful arch ending in inlaid rosettes. The well-placed oval panels above and below the waist door and in the scrollboard draw the design together, leaving no blank areas.

Ht: 92½" Wd: 19¾"
Formerly Israel Sack, Inc.
(whereabouts unknown)

SUPERIOR

Hepplewhite cherry scroll-top clock with inlaid American eagle, made by **John Hoff, Lancaster, Pennsylvania, circa 1810–1820** . This is a choice clock with nice proportions and well-placed inlay. The dramatic American eagle in a large oval adds interest to the design. Comparison of this plainer case with its more exciting companion provides a valuable study.

Ht: 95¾" Wd: 20⅛" Dp: 10¼"
Yale University Art Gallery,
Mabel Brady Garvan Collection

MASTERPIECE

Hepplewhite curly maple scroll-top tall clock with inlaid American eagle by **Jacob Eby, Manheim, Pennsylvania, circa 1810–1820** . There is no question that this and the SUPERIOR clock case was made in the same shop and probably by the same maker, yet the proportions of the hood and the exotic selection of carefully matched striped grain place this clock in another dimension.

Ht: 100½" Wd: 21¼" Dp: 11¼"
From the collections of Henry Ford Museum and Greenfield Village

BETTER

Banjo clock with eglomise glass panels and spiral gilt borders, Massachusetts, circa 1810–1830 **(right).** The banjo clock is an American innovation that has no English prototype. This example is a nice representative clock with average paintings and a boxy base. The proportions are less successful than the SUPERIOR and MASTERPIECE examples.

Whereabouts unknown

SUPERIOR

Banjo clock with eglomise glass panels and cross-banded mahogany borders, made by Simon Willard, Roxbury, Massachusetts, circa 1805–1815 **(below right).** A fine clock by the inventor and patentee of the banjo clock. The proportions are exemplary and the painted glass panels are of excellent quality in the understated taste that Simon Willard preferred.

Formerly Israel Sack, Inc. (whereabouts unknown)

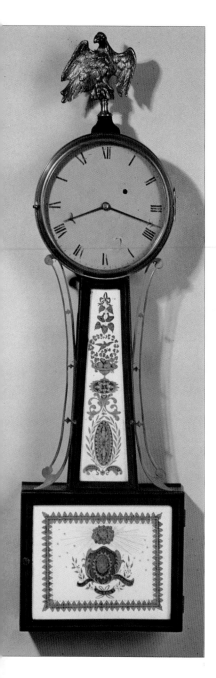

MASTERPIECE

Banjo clock with eglomise glass panels, made by Simon Willard, Roxbury, Massachusetts, circa 1805–1810 **(left).** The brilliant colors and superb artistry of the paints are remarkably preserved and contained on a white background, as is evident in virtually all of Simon Willard's accredited banjo clocks. The original brass eagle is fire-gilded. This clock, along with other masterpieces, was chosen to represent America in the Bicentennial exhibit, organized by the Yale University Art Gallery and the Victoria and Albert Museum in London.

Private collection

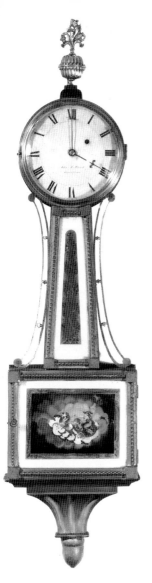

SUPERIOR

Mahogany and gilt banjo clock with original eglomise glass panels, made by John A. Stowell, Charlestown, Massachusetts, circa 1810–1820 (left). A beautifully proportioned clock with a slender waist. The allegoric scene depicting Aurora was a favorite of Aaron Willard, Jr., among other makers.

Ht: 42"
Collection of Dr. and Mrs. David A. Sperling

MASTERPIECE

Mahogany and gilt banjo clock with original eglomise glass panels, unsigned, Boston or Concord, Massachusetts, circa 1810–1820 (right). The eglomise paintings on this banjo clock are among the most beautiful and artistic produced in America. Fortunately, they are contained in an equally beautiful case. The connoisseur properly judges the artistic stature of a clock before the prominence of the maker. Thus we consider this work of art more valuable than many clocks that are signed or definitely attributed.

Ht: 43" Wd: 10¼"   *Private collection*
PHOTOGRAPH: ISRAEL SACK, INC.

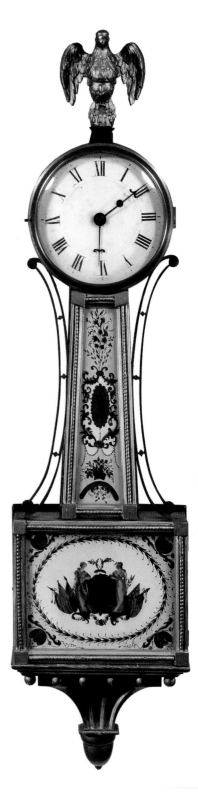

Detail of lower glass panel.

GOOD

Hepplewhite mahogany grandmother clock, made by Joshua Wilder, Hingham, Massachusetts, circa 1810–1820 (right). Joshua Wilder was one of the best-known makers of grandmother clocks, yet he is rated, according to the valid standards taught to me, by the quality of his cases. This example has a squat base, a wide waist, and a small door leaving a large boxy blank area flanking the door.

Whereabouts unknown

BEST

Hepplewhite mahogany grandmother clock, unsigned, probably Hingham, Massachusetts, circa 1810–1820 (below right). The refinement of this case is apparent in the finished craftsmanship, the cross-banded borders of the door and base panel, the ogival molded door border, and the selection of fine mahogany. This unsigned example, judging by the excellence of the case, would be worth more to the connoisseur collector than the signed Joshua Wilder clock rated as GOOD.

Whereabouts unknown

SUPERIOR

Hepplewhite mahogany grandmother clock, made by Joshua Wilder, Hingham, Massachusetts, circa 1810–1820 (left). This case is distinguished by its fine proportion and outstanding selection of highly figured mahogany with cross-banded borders on the door and base. The waist is slenderer than in most examples, which gives the case a feeling of delicacy. The fretwork cresting adds to the appeal. This Wilder clock is worth several times the GOOD example by the same maker.

Formerly Israel Sack, Inc.
(whereabouts unknown)

MASTERPIECE

Hepplewhite mahogany grandmother clock, made by Joshua Wilder, Hingham, Massachusetts, circa 1810–1820. This is the highest level of form achieved in the group of grandmother clocks produced in the Hingham or Hanover area. It vies with the Willard clock cases in sophistication, with its quarter-columns flanking the molded bordered door, the beautiful scrolled apron and flaring feet, and the delicate original fretwork. This will always be recognized as one of the supreme clocks of this rare and desirable group.

Ht: 50¾″ Wd: 10⅞″ Dp: 5½″
Collection of E. Martin

BETTER

Classical mahogany lighthouse clock, signed *S. Willard, Patent Roxbury*; Roxbury, Massachusetts, circa 1820–1835. Any original lighthouse clock by Simon Willard is rare and desirable, and certainly this is no exception. Yet if beauty is a factor, which we strongly believe, the base is boxy and heavy and the waist is too short for proper proportions.

Ht: 28"   *Whereabouts unknown*

MASTERPIECE

Classical bridal lighthouse clock painted white, signed in oval *Simon Willard, Patent Roxbury*; Roxbury, Massachusetts, circa 1820–1830. This is the height of achievement in the limited group of lighthouse clocks, both in its beauty and its original condition. Painted white for presentation to a bride, it retains its original color and glass dome.

Private collection
PHOTOGRAPH: ISRAEL SACK, INC.

SUPERIOR

Classical mahogany pillar-and-scroll shelf clock with thirty-hour wooden works; the label inside reads, *Made and sold at Plymouth, Connecticut, by Eli Terry, Inventor and Patentee*; circa 1820–1825. A choice example by the originator of this popular form. Fortunately, this prolific nineteenth-century group by Terry and many of his contemporaries retained the delicate design of the earlier Hepplewhite period.

Ht: 31¼" Wd: 16½" Dp: 4"   Israel Sack, Inc.

MASTERPIECE

Classical mahogany pillar-and-scroll shelf clock with ivory decoration, inside-outside escapement with thirty-hour wooden works, made by Eli Terry, Plymouth, Massachusetts, circa 1819. Eli Terry elevated his standard model to a creative work of art. The pierced open fretwork accented by the ivory inlaid motifs is a brilliant and exotic original design. The case is framed by columns and borders of curly maple. The original wooden works have an inside escapement mechanism, which is rare and highly prized by clock collectors.

Ht: 28" Wd: 17½" Dp: 4½"   Israel Sack, Inc.

DESKS

BETTER

Queen Anne applewood desk-on-frame, Pennsylvania, circa 1740–1760. Only a small number of desks-on-frame survived with the frames intact, so any such example is a rarity. However, the cabriole legs on this example are stiff and not too well integrated with the frame.

Ht: 42½" Wd: 36" Dp: 21"
Whereabouts unknown

SUPERIOR

Queen Anne maple desk-on-frame, Massachusetts, circa 1740–1760. A compact, beautifully proportioned gem. The silhouette formed by the graceful cyma-shaped apron with the ridged bandy cabriole legs is inspirational.

Ht: 39" Wd: 26" Dp: 18"
Collection of Mr. and Mrs. George M. Kaufman

BETTER

Queen Anne cherry desk-on-frame with cabriole legs ending in pad feet, Connecticut, circa 1750–1770. A country version that has small size and rural charm to favor its rating. The apron is not refined and the interior is relatively simple. The cabriole legs are nicely modeled.

Ht: 40½" Wd: 31½"

PHOTOGRAPHIC ARCHIVES, NATIONAL GALLERY OF ART

BEST

Queen Anne birch desk with cabriole legs ending in platformed pad feet, Massachusetts, circa 1750–1770. The interior of this desk is rated well above average due to its fan-carved center drawer and convex end drawers. The platformed pad feet have a somewhat abrupt turn of the ankles.

Ht: 42" Wd: 41"

PHOTOGRAPHIC ARCHIVES, NATIONAL GALLERY OF ART

MASTERPIECE

Queen Anne cherry desk with cabriole legs ending in platformed pad feet, Massachusetts, circa 1750–1770. This desk shows the creative imagination of a skilled designer combined with excellent craftsmanship. The interior is formed by complex rows of concave and convex blocked drawers centered by fan-and-spiral-rosette-carved motifs. The cabriole legs are finely modeled and the cyma shaping of the knee brackets is repeated on the central pendant. The desk lid is centered by a compass star inlay.

Ht: 43½" Wd: 38" Dp: 18½"
Courtesy Honolulu Academy of Arts

BETTER

Chippendale mahogany kneehole desk with ogee bracket feet, Maryland, circa 1760–1780. This is a simple but well-crafted example of a scarce American form. The ogee bracket feet seem too small to create a harmonious balance with the case.

Ht: 29" Wd: 36" Dp: 20"
Whereabouts unknown

MASTERPIECE

Chippendale mahogany carved kneehole desk, Philadelphia, circa 1760–1780. This is probably the most highly developed example of a handful of Philadelphia kneehole desks known. The first-rank carving is skillfully placed to accent the form without overpowering it. The ogee bracket feet are gadrooned and acanthus carved and relate to those on a rococo Philadelphia secretary (see *American Furniture from the Kaufman Collection,* The National Gallery of Art, 1986, plate 31). The chased bail brasses and the fretwork frieze under the top are effective refinements.

Ht: 32¾" Wd: 31½" Dp: 21½"   *Collection of June and Joseph Hennage*

MASTERPIECE

Chippendale walnut desk, Chester County, Pennsylvania, 1771. An outstanding example of Pennsylvania German art. The bird motifs above the date 1771 on the slant lid are ivory. The star motifs in circles are symbolic. The interior with ogival blocked drawers and inlaid patterns (below) is equally dramatic. According to family tradition, this desk was made by Jacob Reese, cabinetmaker and joiner for his son Philip Reese. JACOB REESE is branded below the date.

Ht: 44" Wd: 38¼" Dp: 20" Wr. lev: 31"   *Private collection*

PHOTOGRAPH: ISRAEL SACK, INC.

*Detail: view of well
and ladder interior.*

MASTERPIECE

William and Mary walnut and crotch walnut veneered ball-foot desk, Massachusetts,
circa 1710–1730. This desk excels from every standpoint. The trumpet-shaped ball feet
are finely turned. The crotch walnut veneer is outlined by herringbone borders and the four
crotch panels of the lid accentuate the verticality. The blocked drawers of the "well and ladder" interior is a refinement.

Ht: 40½" Wd: 35¾" Dp: 20½"
Private collection

BETTER

Chippendale mahogany block-front kneehole desk or bureau table with claw and ball feet, New York, circa 1760–1780. Only a few New York block-front kneehole desks are known, and all that have surfaced have typical squared claw and ball feet, as does this one. To my eye and that of many connoisseurs, the massive feet overpower the case and do not continue the line of the blocking as do the Massachusetts examples.

Whereabouts unknown

BEST

Queen Anne–Chippendale mahogany block-front kneehole desk or bureau table with bracket feet, Massachusetts, circa 1740–1750. Hundreds of these pleasing kneehole desks were fashioned in the seacoast centers of Massachusetts, and they outnumber the more ambitious Newport group with shells by at least ten to one. They exhibit the same harmony of form and integration and are usually similar in size to the Massachusetts block-front bureaus. Since the knee space is too small for practical use, it may have been built for a storage function. The blocking and other features of this kneehole are not as bold or brilliant as on the comparative MASTERPIECE.

Formerly Israel Sack, Inc.
(whereabouts unknown)

MASTERPIECE

Queen Anne–Chippendale block-front kneehole desk or bureau table with bracket feet, Boston or Salem, Massachusetts, circa 1740–1760. A compact little gem with bold, compressed round blocking. This type of narrow blocking and the arched paneled door reflect an earlier influence. The narrow proportions and the tall, arched central compartment accentuate the desk's strong sense of verticality and result in a completely successful overall work.

Ht: 31" Wd: 32" Dp: 20½"   *Private collection*

MASTERPIECE

Chippendale mahogany block-and-shell-carved kneehole desk or bureau table, Goddard-Townsend group, attributed to Edmund Townsend, Newport, Rhode Island, circa 1760–1770. The forty or fifty known kneehole desks of this form, along with the several block-and-shell secretaries, are considered the supreme achievements of New England artisans in the Chippendale era. This four-shell example, known as the Gibbs kneehole, stands along with the top five or six examples of its class by virtue of its quality of carving, condition, and golden color. The complexity of the challenges of integration solved in this design are belied by the apparent simplicity and directness of the form. The panels of the blocking flow from the superbly carved shells through the ogival base moldings and continue in a bulged ogee foot bracket ending in a scrolled volute. The outline of the foot bracket moves downward in a straight path to continue the straight line of the edges of the blocked panels and thus does not follow the s-shaped outer outline of the bracket foot. A coved retaining molding unites the molded top to the case. Even the bulged continuations of the knee returns unite and follow along the base and sides of the cupboard section.

Ht: 33¼" Wd: 35" Dp: 19"   Collection of Erving and Joyce Wolf

PHOTOGRAPH: ISRAEL SACK, INC.

BETTER

Chippendale mahogany claw-and-ball-foot block-front desk with blocked lid and fan-carved center, Massachusetts, circa 1760–1780. This truly outstanding desk of the finest craftsmanship has, for some inexplicable reason, squared knees that are a jarring design aberration.

Whereabouts unknown

Detail of open view. The interior is outstanding and typical of the group.

MASTERPIECE

Chippendale mahogany block-front desk with blocked lid and blocked amphitheater interior, Salem, Massachusetts, circa 1760–1780. Several related desks with the distinctive convex shell pendant can definitely be ascribed to Salem. The extension of the blocking on the lid provides a powerful vertical paneled effect. The carved knees are a rare feature.

Ht: 43" Wd: 41¾" Dp: 22"   Private collection

BETTER

Chippendale mahogany slant-top desk, Massachusetts, circa 1760–1780. A fine-quality desk showing excellent craftsmanship, choice grained mahogany, and a simple but competent interior. Its broad width is practical but not as appealing as other compact examples.

Ht: 42" Wd: 43" Dp: 22½"
Whereabouts unknown

SUPERIOR

Chippendale walnut slant-top desk, Massachusetts, circa 1760–1780. The compact size results in a fine proportion. The choice interior cabinet, with concave and convex blocked drawers and fan-carved center and end sections, serves to make this an outstanding example. The bracket feet are a perfect height and breadth to blend with the narrow proportion of the case.

Ht: 42¼" Wd: 36" Dp: 19"   Private collection

MASTERPIECE

Chippendale mahogany block-front slant-top desk, Boston, circa 1760–1780. An outstanding specimen that exudes power and virility with no sacrifice to grace. The bold squared blocking is accentuated by equally bold and rare brasses which appear on a handful of Boston block-front pieces. The interior is fully blocked and fan carved with flame pilasters and scooped pigeonhole drawers that show a strong Newport association. The spurs of the center pendant complement the spurred outlines of the foot brackets.

Ht: 43" Wd: 41" Dp: 22⅓"   *Private collection*

BETTER

C**hippendale mahogany oxbow claw-and-ball-foot desk, Massachusetts, circa 1780–1800.** The oxbow claw-and-ball-foot desk was made in considerable quantity, particularly in North Shore centers of Massachusetts. Many of these desks in the Chippendale form continued to be made up to 1800. The original oval brasses here suggest a post-Revolutionary origin. This example has a weak curve and an uninteresting plain interior.

Formerly collection of Charles K. Davis (whereabouts unknown)

BEST

C**hippendale mahogany oxbow claw-and-ball-foot desk, Massachusetts, circa 1760–1790.** A more compact example with a fine fan-carved interior. The cyma-shaped knee brackets and center pendant help prevent the monotony of a plain base.

Ht: 45½″ Wd: 41½″ Dp: 21½″
Whereabouts unknown
PHOTOGRAPH: ISRAEL SACK, INC.

SUPERIOR

C**hippendale mahogany oxbow claw-and-ball-foot desk, Massachusetts, signed and dated by Nathaniel Bowen, 19th September, 1780.** The blocked row of drawers in the interior, plus the fine center door with ogival panel and document drawers, result in a choice interior rarely seen in serpentine-front desks. The claw and ball feet are finely sculptured with knobby knuckles and swept-back (retractable) talons.

Ht: 44″ Wd: 46¾″ Dp: 23″
COURTESY OF CHRISTIE'S

SUPERIOR-
MASTERPIECE

Chippendale mahogany block-front desk with block-and-shell-carved lid, freestanding rope columns, Connecticut, circa 1760–1800. Nothing expresses the bold and daring free spirit of the Connecticut innovators better than this creation. Even though it violates most rules of academic convention, it exudes power. The center shell is different from the end shells. The rope columns and wide bracket feet are massive.

Ht: 47" Wd: 44¾" Dp: 27"
From the collections of Henry Ford Museum and Greenfield Village

PHOTOGRAPH: ISRAEL SACK, INC.

Detail: the label of John Townsend, located in the first long drawer of the desk.

MASTERPIECE

Chippendale mahogany block-and-shell-carved slant-top desk made and labeled by John Townsend, Newport, Rhode Island, 1765. Given the number of major Newport block-and-shell forms, the slant-top desk is represented by relatively few known examples. It is fortunate, therefore, that this example, the finest of the group, is documented as the work of John Townsend. The superbly carved shells by this master conform to those seen on other labeled John Townsend pieces and establish his standing as perhaps the most gifted Newport artisan. It is interesting to contrast the proportions of this desk with the comparative Connecticut example. The Newport desk is more compact, as can be seen by the measurements and the refinement of craftsmanship. The carving and interior development is exemplary.

Ht: 42" Wd: 42" Dp: 23"   *Collection of Mr. and Mrs. Stanley P. Sax*
PHOTOGRAPH: ISRAEL SACK, INC.

BETTER

Chippendale mahogany slant-top desk, Newport, Rhode Island, circa 1760–1780. A compact, nicely proportioned desk. The ogee bracket feet are somewhat undeveloped. The interior is of a quality not to be criticized, but is rather simple.

Whereabouts unknown

PHOTOGRAPH: JOHN HOPF

BEST

Chippendale mahogany slant-top desk, Goddard-Townsend school, Newport, Rhode Island, circa 1760–1780. A fine representative of the standard Newport desk. The ogee bracket feet are of typical Newport formation with the straight inner edge but are slightly broad for the proportion of the case. The interior has a bottom row of convex and concave drawer blocking and a typical Rhode Island center shell.

Ht: 41½" Wd: 37½" Dp: 21½"
Whereabouts unknown

MASTERPIECE

Chippendale mahogany slant-top desk with block-and-shell-carved interior signed by John Goddard, 1754, Newport, Rhode Island. The choice proportion, craftsmanship, and superb interior of this documented example reinforces the reputation of John Goddard as a first-rank master craftsman.

Ht: 41½" Wd: 40½" Dp: 21½"
Private collection

BETTER

Hepplewhite mahogany inlaid tambour desk with bellflower drapery inlaid tambour shutters, school of John Seymour and Son, Boston, circa 1785–1800. This desk is related to the labeled MASTERPIECE example. However, the boxiness of the base section overpowers the delicacy and successful proportion of the tambour section.

Ht: 46½" Wd: 41¼"   Whereabouts unknown

MASTERPIECE

Hepplewhite mahogany inlaid tambour desk with bellflower drapery inlaid tambour shutters, authenticated to the shop of John Seymour and Son, Boston, circa 1785–1800. While not labeled, this desk is virtually identical to the labeled example at the Winterthur Museum. It is one of several related examples that establish the reputation of John Seymour as the supreme cabinetmaker of New England in the Federal period. The overall design and delicate proportion, the beautiful detail of the drapery-bellflower inlay, and superb craftsmanship serve to place this desk in the MASTERPIECE category.

Ht: 51½" Wd: 37½" Dp: 19½"   The Cleveland Museum of Art, Leonard C. Hanna, Jr., Fund, 87.11
PHOTOGRAPH: ISRAEL SACK, INC.

MASTERPIECE

Hepplewhite mahogany rolltop desk with inlaid American eagle, Baltimore, circa 1790–1810. A magnificent interpretation of a form that could only achieve fluency in the hands of a master designer. The proud eagle, symbol of our new independence, provides the focus on an otherwise broad expanse. The base is equally well handled with a graceful apron veneered with satinwood panels.

Ht: 44¼" Wd: 42½" Dp: 21½" Writing height: 33¼"   *The Art Institute of Chicago*
Gift of the Antiquarian Society through Joy Martin Brown, Mrs. Harold T. Martin, Mrs. Edgar J. Yihlein, and Melinda Martin Vance.
PHOTOGRAPH: ISRAEL SACK, INC.

SECRETARIES

BETTER

Chippendale mahogany block-front secretary-desk, Massachusetts, circa 1760–1780. A fine secretary in every respect except proportion. The top case section does not have enough height in relation to the base. A comparison with the SUPERIOR secretary emphasizes this weakness.

Whereabouts unknown
PHOTOGRAPHIC ARCHIVES, NATIONAL GALLERY OF ART

SUPERIOR

Chippendale mahogany block-front secretary-desk, Massachusetts, circa 1760–1780. The vertical proportion of this secretary epitomizes the colonial emphasis. There is little question that the cabinetmaker was also a draftsman capable of achieving a successful ratio of height versus width. The block-and-fan-carved desk interior is similar to that of the BETTER secretary.

Ht: 93" Wd: 40" Dp: 22
Whereabouts unknown

BETTER

Chippendale cherry secretary-desk, New Jersey or Pennsylvania, circa 1770–1800 (right). A rural secretary only 38" wide. The bonnet is weak and has a small arch opening. The claw and ball feet are not integrated to the base and only a physical examination would determine their originality to the case.

Ht: 91" Wd: 38"   Whereabouts unknown

PHOTOGRAPHIC ARCHIVES, NATIONAL GALLERY OF ART

BETTER-BEST

Chippendale mahogany secretary-desk, New London County, Connecticut, circa 1760–1780 (left). The use of slender vertical proportions, so favored in most East Coast centers, was not followed in this instance. This important offshoot of Newport's Goddard-Townsend school followed the English preference. The bonnet has the same magnificent moldings and panels of the Townsend examples, but by spreading it out to encompass the width it becomes squarish and less fluent. Except for fans replacing shells, the interior is the same as on many Goddard-Townsend desks and secretaries.

Ht: 96½" Wd: 50½" Dp: 24⅞"

COURTESY OF SUFFOLK COUNTY HISTORICAL SOCIETY

MASTERPIECE

Chippendale mahogany secretary-desk ascribed to John Townsend, Newport, Rhode Island, circa 1760–1780 (made for Jonathan Nichols, who owned the White Horse Tavern) (right). The stature of American furniture does not always depend on ornament or motifs. From the standpoint of perfect proportion, design craftsmanship, and original condition and surface, this secretary ranks among the great Newport productions. Comparison of this interior to the labeled John Townsend desk proves its authorship. The divided blocked panels of the scrollboard line up with the doors of the upper section to integrate these elements.

Ht: 98" Wd: 40½" Dp: 23"   Private collection

MASTERPIECE

Chippendale mahogany block-and-shell-carved secretary, Goddard-Townsend craftsmanship, Newport, Rhode Island, circa 1760–1770 (made for Nicholas Brown of Providence, Rhode Island).** If one piece were to be selected to represent the contribution of the American furniture craftsmen, this masterpiece would have few rivals. Its magnificent stateliness and towering proportions epitomize the preference of the colonial artisan for the vertical emphasis. This secretary is one of nine known six-shell examples. The six-shell secretary was the crowning achievement of the Goddard-Townsend cabinetmaking families of Newport. At least one was made for each of the four Brown brothers. Nicholas Brown was one of the four brothers. It is a masterpiece of integration. In order to make the blocking of the doors follow the three-paneled blocking of the desk drawer and lid, one door forms a hinged folding door containing a convex and concave blocked panel, enabling the two doors to form three panels when closed.

Ht: 113" Wd: 42⅝" Dp: 25"
Private collection

PHOTOGRAPHS: ISRAEL SACK, INC.

Open view: The block-and-shell-carved interior with scooped drawer pigeonhole terminals is found in desks of Goddard-Townsend authorship. The upper interior shows the folding door and the adjustable shelves to hold books.

BETTER

Chippendale mahogany bombe secretary-desk with hairy paw feet, Boston, circa 1760–1770. What could have been a masterpiece is downgraded by rather clumsy hairy paw feet and a stiff arch. Comparison of the arch with the corresponding MASTERPIECE is useful.

Ht: 99" Wd: 42"   *Whereabouts unknown*

PHOTOGRAPH: ISRAEL SACK, INC.

MASTERPIECE

Chippendale mahogany bombe secretary-desk with claw and ball feet and eagle ornaments, Boston or Springfield, Massachusetts, circa 1770–1780. In the hands of a skilled craftsman, the bombe base is in excellent proportion, with no feeling of mass or bulk. The carved mahogany eagle ornaments are unique and crown a supreme achievement. Two or three related secretaries with glass doors are attributed to Springfield. The San Domingan dense mahogany and the urban sophistication of this piece suggest a Boston origin.

Ht: 99" Wd: 46"   *Private collection*

BETTER

Chippendale walnut scroll-top secretary-desk, Pennsylvania, circa 1760–1780. Though this secretary has some strong points, particularly the deeply chamfered arched door panels, the crest fades into a thin, swanlike scrolled pediment. The ogee feet are small and out of scale with the weight of the piece. The interior is simple, relieved somewhat by the shell-carved center door.

© 1956, SOTHEBY'S, INC.

MASTERPIECE

Chippendale walnut scroll-top secretary-desk, Philadelphia, circa 1760–1780. A superb example, exhibiting the skill, proportion, carving, and craftsmanship of a top-rank Philadelphia artisan. The arch moldings end in finely carved terminals; the scrollboard is fronted by a pierced carved shell and vines capped by a rhythmic carved cartouche. The arched door panels of richly figured grain have carved borders. The blocked ogival interior and the finely modeled ogee feet are fitting to its rating. The importance of this creation is enhanced by the relative scarcity of fine Philadelphia secretaries.

PHILADELPHIA MUSEUM OF ART

BETTER

Chippendale mahogany block-front secretary-desk with broken-arch top, Massachusetts, circa 1760–1780 **(right).** The proportions of this secretary are broad and squarish. This emphasis is compounded by the broad, flat expanse flanking the skimpy ogival door panels. The flattened arch adds to the squareness of the design.

Whereabouts unknown

PHOTOGRAPHIC ARCHIVES, NATIONAL GALLERY OF ART

MASTERPIECE

Chippendale mahogany block-front block-lid secretary-desk, signed by John Chipman, Salem, Massachusetts, circa 1770–1790 **(left).** This magnificent interpretation vies with the great block-and-shell secretaries of Newport. The blocking is bold and dramatic, and its continuation on the slant lid adds to the verticality as well as to the integration. The ogival panels have a deep chamfer which creates a boldness compatible with the blocking. The spurred flourish on the majestic arch, repeated on the base pendant, reflects the romantic tendency of Salem craftsmen. Because so few Salem craftsmen of this stature have been identified, the signature of John Chipman as the cabinetmaker is of the utmost importance. (For an article on John Chipman, by Donald R. Sack and Peter Louis, see *Antiques,* December 1987, page 1318.)

Ht: 95" Wd: 45¼" Dp: 23⅔"
Private collection

PHOTOGRAPH: ISRAEL SACK, INC.

BEST

Chippendale cherry pediment-top secretary-desk, Connecticut Valley, circa 1780–1800. A pleasing, high country secretary of good proportion. The elements and interior are simple, yet the ogee bracket feet and ogival paneled doors are well modeled. The fan inlay in the cornice eliminates blandness.

Whereabouts unknown
PHOTOGRAPH: ISRAEL SACK, INC.

Detail of open view.

MASTERPIECE

Chippendale cherry pediment-top secretary-desk, Connecticut, circa 1775–1795. It is hard to find superlatives to describe this tour de force of Connecticut innovative genius. The magnificent blocked amphitheater interior is contained in a diminutive case with bold oxbow blocking, flanked by fluted quarter-columns with brass capitals. The fretted frieze and pediment are outlined in black, and a proud, primitive gilt eagle boasts the achievement.

Ht: 89" Wd: 39" Dp: 21"   *Private collection*

Detail of open view.

SUPERIOR-MASTERPIECE

Hepplewhite applewood china cabinet, Maryland, circa 1780–1800. A beautifully proportioned vertical example with a graceful arch enclosing a rhythmic open-fretwork scrollboard. The case is signed *Laws*, which may refer to William Laws, a cabinetmaker in Montgomery County, Maryland.

Ht: 98¼" Wd: 41" Dp: 20"   Collection of Mrs. Robert K. Moses, Jr.

BETTER

S heraton mahogany secretary-desk with Gothic glass doors, circa 1800–1820 (left). Because of a subtle difference in proportion, this secretary-desk lacks delicacy in comparison with the SUPERIOR examples. The multiple turnings of the legs lack the same refinement, and the scroll top does not work as well on this form as on earlier examples.

Whereabouts unknown

SUPERIOR

S heraton mahogany secretary-desk with Gothic glass doors, Boston, circa 1800–1815 (right). A beautiful example with fine proportion and a balance between the elements. The figured birch of the lid panel is repeated on the drawers above, adding appealing touches to the façade. The tapered, reeded legs are more refined than on the BETTER example.

Ht: 84" Wd: 37½" *Whereabouts unknown*

PHOTOGRAPHIC ARCHIVES, NATIONAL GALLERY OF ART

MASTERPIECE

S heraton mahogany and satinwood secretary-desk with Gothic glass doors, attributed to John Seymour, Boston, circa 1800–1815. Only a master craftsman of the caliber of John Seymour could create this chef d'oeuvre. Every element serves the master touch, beginning with its small scale and perfect proportion. The refinement of the swelled and tapered reeded legs and ringed bulbous feet combine with scrolled spandrels and the ringed plinths to form a beautiful support for the lower case. The satinwood fronts were used by few craftsmen other than Seymour, figured birch being more common. The twin row of divided drawers integrates the secretary top to the lower case and serves as a base for the figured satinwood or birch plinths that support reeded mullions housing eglomise glass panels.

Ht: 78½" Wd: 38½" Dp: 22"
Courtesy of the Colonial Williamsburg Foundation, Williamsburg, Virginia

PHOTOGRAPH: ISRAEL SACK, INC.

BETTER

Hepplewhite mahogany glass-door secretary-desk, Massachusetts, circa 1790–1810 (right). This secretary exhibits very fine quality, craftsmanship, and selection of figured mahogany. Its weakness lies in the abbreviated height of the top case in relation to the base section. The ideal proportion is apparent in the MASTERPIECE.

Whereabouts unknown
PHOTOGRAPH: ISRAEL SACK, INC.

SUPERIOR

Hepplewhite mahogany glass-door secretary-desk with inlaid American eagle in plinth, Boston, circa 1810–1815 (left). The reduction in width of the upper case with the lower case results in a more pleasing pyramidal effect. This secretary is small in scale, and its importance is enhanced by the highly prized eagle inlay. The height of the upper case in relation to the lower case is adequate, but the MASTERPIECE has more emphasis on the vertical thrust.

Ht: 77½" Wd: 40" Dp: 20"
Private collection

Detail of crest.

MASTERPIECE

Hepplewhite mahogany glass-door secretary-desk with inlaid American eagle in plinth, Boston, circa 1810–1815. If one piece had to be chosen to represent the American eagle inlay in American furniture, this would be one of my favorites. It is the embodiment of vertical proportion and perfect ratio of top to base. The figured birch panels, including the oval fronting the desk drawer, the excitement of the eagle plinth, surmounted by the beautiful brass eagle holding one olive branch, and the original mellow patina combine to make this a chef d'oeuvre.

Ht: 85" Wd: 43" Dp: 21¼"
Private collection

PHOTOGRAPH: ISRAEL SACK, INC.

BETTER

Hepplewhite cherry inlaid linen press with American eagle inlay, New York or New Jersey, circa 1800–1820. Any piece with the inlaid symbol of our new Republic is significant, but the rules of fine craftsmanship and design still follow. Compared with the following MASTERPIECE, the base is relatively crude, the proportions are square and boxy, and the crest is not refined.

Whereabouts unknown

MASTERPIECE

Hepplewhite mahogany inlaid linen press with American eagle inlay, New York, circa 1800–1815. A gifted craftsman transformed a functional storage piece into a work of art. Magnificent in its proportion and craftsmanship, it boasts not one American eagle but three, in diamond or rectangular satinwood fields. The base, with outsplayed feet and scrolled apron, is the epitome of grace, as is the crest, with its brass eagle finials.

Ht: 84" Wd: 45" Dp: 21"   *Private collection*

MASTERPIECE

Hepplewhite mahogany inlaid breakfront bookcase with eglomise glass panels, Massachusetts, circa 1780–1810. This supreme American bookcase is now recognized as a priceless American gem. Israel Sack recognized it early in his career. By 1915 or 1920, Israel Sack had already become the leading dealer in Boston. One day Helen Temple Cooke, the wealthy dean of Dana Hall, Wellesley, drove up to my father's shop in her chauffeured limousine and said, "Mr. Sack, I know of your reputation, and I want you to get some of the *very, very best* antiques and I will pay you a *very, very* good price." Israel Sack replied, "Miss Cooke, you are the lady of the hour," and he sold her this magnificent, much-copied bookcase for $2,500. Just before the Depression, in 1928 or 1929, she called Israel Sack and said, "Mr. Sack, I've decided to sell some of my *very, very* best antiques, but I want a *very, very* good price." She sold my father the bookcase for $20,000. He sold it to Mr. du Pont and it is now on display at Winterthur.

Ht: 92½" Wd: 75¼" Dp: 22½"   ***Courtesy of Winterthur Museum***

MASTERPIECE

Hepplewhite mahogany breakfront bookcase with oval mirrored doors, Baltimore, circa 1780–1800. One of the most beautiful of America's small group of breakfront bookcases. The oval mirrors center glass doors of Gothic-shaped inlaid mullions. Below the drop-lid desk are drawers with Battersea or Bilsted handles and document compartments.

Ht: 91" Wd: 86" Dp: 22½"   Private collection

PHOTOGRAPH: ISRAEL SACK, INC.

HIGHBOYS

BEST-SUPERIOR

William and Mary highboy with crotch veneered front, inverted cup and trumpet turnings, Massachusetts, circa 1710–1740. A standard high-quality highboy. The wealthier families in the centers of New England and occasionally New York would ornament the fronts with carefully selected crotch veneer or burl with herringbone borders. The percentage of original bases that survived intact is extremely small. Note that the arch and pointed-arch outline of the beaded apron are repeated on the stretcher plane.

Whereabouts unknown
PHOTOGRAPH: ISRAEL SACK, INC.

MASTERPIECE

William and Mary highboy with crotch walnut front, inverted cup and trumpet turnings, Massachusetts, circa 1710–1740 (belonged to Timothy Pickering, George Washington's secretary of state and author of the Pickering papers). A jewel. It excels in compact proportion, condition, and magnificent patina. The refined inverted cup-turned trumpet legs are ebonized. The teardrop brasses secured by cotter pins are original. The premium stature of this "Pickering" highboy makes it worth several times that of the comparable standard high-quality highboy.

Ht: 61¾" Wd: 39" Dp: 22"
Collection of Erving and Joyce Wolf

ENGLISH

Early Queen Anne crotch walnut ve-neered front tallboy, England, circa **1710–1740.** In England the highboy form was called a tallboy. Both are vernacular though popular descriptions. The English tallboy hardly got off the ground because the English probably did not want to sacrifice drawer usage for high legs. The broad, or horizontal, emphasis is typically English.

Whereabouts unknown

AMERICAN: SUPERIOR

Early Queen Anne crotch walnut ve-neered front highboy, Massachusetts, circa **1720–1740.** The colonists' love for vertical proportions caused them to sacrifice utility for beauty, so they lifted the high chest on tall graceful legs. Notice the lift created by the high arch of the apron. Also, note the narrower vertical proportion of this typical New England example.

Ht: 67½" Wd: 37" Dp: 21"
Private collection

MASTERPIECE example
appears on page 184.

Detail of lowboy top: The skillful matching of the quartered crotch-veneered sections of the lowboy top with its herringbone and cross-banded borders shows the demand of the clients for fine craftsmanship combined with graceful form.

MASTERPIECE

Early Queen Anne highboy and companion lowboy, crotch walnut veneered front with herringbone borders made for Ebenezer Gay, Salem, Massachusetts, circa 1735–1740. This highboy, with its matching lowboy, was purchased by Israel Sack from the Gay estate in 1915. Early in his career, Israel Sack recognized the graceful form and beauty of the New England Queen Anne expressions and their differences from English prototypes. The high arch of the center apron, outlined with beaded strips, and the smoothly curved cabriole legs add lift to the case and emphasize the vertical proportion so admired throughout the cabriole period in the colonies. The foresight of Israel Sack in recognizing the greatness of this superb Queen Anne combination is inspirational. He sold the set to Albert Whittier for about $500. In 1957 we repurchased the highboy and lowboy combination and sold it to Joseph Hirschhorn for $10,000. We repurchased the set from the Hirschhorn estate in 1981 for over $200,000 and it is now in a private collection. This dramatic increase shows the growing recognition of American Queen Anne as a major art form.

Highboy: Ht: 68" Wd: 37½" Dp: 20"   Lowboy: Ht: 30½" Wd: 33¼" Dp: 21"
Private collection

BETTER

Queen Anne curly maple highboy, Massachusetts, circa 1740–1760 (left). This highboy is distinguished by the exceptionally figured curly grain, yet its stature is diminished by the broad underslung lower case, which does not integrate well with the upper case section.

Whereabouts unknown

PHOTOGRAPHIC ARCHIVES, NATIONAL GALLERY OF ART

SUPERIOR

Queen Anne curly maple highboy, Massachusetts, circa 1740–1760 (right). A finely proportioned highboy with choice curly striped figuring. Note the more successful integration of the upper and lower case sections.

Ht: 74" Wd: 37½"
Whereabouts unknown

PHOTOGRAPHIC ARCHIVES, NATIONAL GALLERY OF ART

MASTERPIECE

Queen Anne curly maple highboy, made by Moses Bayley and Joshua Morss, Newbury, Massachusetts, 1747. This duo of gifted artisans took the standard form of highboy, as represented by the SUPERIOR example, to exalted heights. By slightly reducing the scale, and by thinning the exquisitely graceful cabriole legs with a high arched apron, they achieved in simplicity what many artisans could not do with ornament. The cotter pins securing the original engraved brasses have never been disturbed.

Ht: 71" Wd: 36½" Dp: 19½"
Private collection

BETTER

Queen Anne curly maple slipper-foot highboy, Newport, Rhode Island, circa 1740–1760. The weakness of this otherwise fine highboy is the angular squared cabriole legs which appear to be placed into the case as an afterthought.

Ht: 67½" Wd: 38¼" Dp: 21½"

© 1991, SOTHEBY'S, INC.

BEST

Queen Anne mahogany slipper-foot highboy attributed to one of the Townsends, Newport, Rhode Island, circa 1740–1760. The drafting skill that became the norm in Goddard-Townsend craftsmanship is apparent in this typical early model. The silhouette of the base, which emanates in three planes from the point of the slipper foot along the ridges of the squared cabriole legs to the graceful front and side aprons and the corners of the lower case, shows the mastery of architectural harmony.

Ht: 80" Wd: 38½" Dp: 20½"
Formerly Israel Sack, Inc.
(whereabouts unknown)

MASTERPIECE

Queen Anne mahogany slipper-foot highboy attributed to one of the Townsends, Newport, Rhode Island, circa 1740–1760. My favorite highboy of this group. The refinements are subtle. The slenderizing of the squared cabriole, the trim line of the apron silhouette, the compactness and perfect proportion of the case, and the use of a top row of three drawers to tighten the composition make this piece "poetry in motion." This highboy was apportioned by George Hussey to Clothier Pierce of Newport in his inventory of 1770 at a value of 2-pounds-10.

Ht: 72" Wd: 39" Dp: 21"   *Private collection*

BETTER

Queen Anne highboy, Rhode Island or Long Island, circa 1730–1750. Transitional features from the William and Mary period are suggested by the apron outline, the bulged bolster drawer, and the engraved cotter pin brasses. The piece sags somewhat in its short cabriole legs abetted by the broader proportion of the upper case.

© SOTHEBY'S, INC.

SUPERIOR-MASTERPIECE

Queen Anne walnut highboy, Long Island, circa 1730–1750. While the base is broad with the early overhanging mid-moldings, the proportions of this piece are dramatic but successful. The cyma curves and coves of the overhanging cornice balance the mid-moldings. The proportion is aided by a smoothly rounded knee and a higher cabriole leg. The superior original nut-brown patina is an additional asset. A related highboy is attributed to an Oyster Bay, Long Island, craftsman in Dean F. Failey's *Long Island Is My Nation* (1976), Plate 136. The relationship of Newport and Long Island design elements is documented.

Ht: 69" Wd: 40½" Dp: 21¼"
Private collection

BETTER

Queen Anne cherry highboy, Connecticut, circa 1750–1780 (left). Neither the thick legs nor the platformed feet lift this highboy enough to keep it from being heavy. The proportions are somewhat square. With those exceptions, it has some fine qualities, including the rare dressing slide.

Whereabouts unknown
PHOTOGRAPHIC ARCHIVES, NATIONAL GALLERY OF ART

BETTER

Queen Anne cherry highboy, Connecticut, circa 1750–1780 (right). A fine example with rare but flattened Spanish feet. Its weakness is a stiff leg with little or no bend.

Whereabouts unknown
PHOTOGRAPHIC ARCHIVES, NATIONAL GALLERY OF ART

MASTERPIECE

Queen Anne cherry highboy, Connecticut, circa 1750–1780. If there were a list of candidates for MASTERPIECE category among Connecticut flat-top highboys, this would be high on the list. The knee brackets with their little scrolled volutes add an elegant touch to the beautiful silhouette of the high-perched base. The proportions and ratio of height to width approach perfection. The row of four drawers under the fan-carved drawer serves to develop the vertical emphasis. The old or original finish is appealing.

Ht: 72" Wd: 37½" Dp: 20¼"
Private collection

BETTER

Queen Anne maple highboy, Rhode Island, circa 1740–1760. The cabriole leg does not have enough lift and has too long a thigh which thins out only when it reaches the ankle. The lack of divided drawers under the cornice is relatively dull compared to the SUPERIOR example.

Whereabouts unknown

SUPERIOR

Queen Anne cherry highboy, Newport, Rhode Island, circa 1740–1760. Beauty in simplicity is here aided by a choice amber patina not visible in the photograph. The proportion is exemplary, yet the case is more of a squared ratio, characteristic of Rhode Island case pieces. The divided top row of drawers serves to unify the design. The ankles thrust to the center of the pad in the Newport manner and the removable legs are also typical. The apron silhouette far surpasses the BETTER example.

Ht: 74" Wd: 40" Dp: 19"
Formerly Israel Sack, Inc.
(whereabouts unknown)

BETTER

Queen Anne curly maple drake-foot highboy, Philadelphia or Delaware Valley, Pennsylvania, circa 1750–1770. This fine quality highboy has beautifully figured curly grain but is built too low to the ground. The deep single drawer in the lower case loses the unity offered by the conventional drawer arrangement.

Ht: 71¾" Wd: 42½"

© 1991, SOTHEBY'S, INC.

BEST

Queen Anne mahogany claw-and-ball-foot highboy, Philadelphia, circa 1750–1770. The competent craftsmanship and refinement of this model points to its Philadelphia origin. The chamfered fluted corners, the shell-and-flower-carved knees and c-scrolled borders relate to the SUPERIOR counterpart and suggest possible common authorship. The brasses on both pieces are similar. The legs do not have as smooth a curve nor the upper case the verticality of the SUPERIOR counterpart.

Whereabouts unknown

PHOTOGRAPHIC ARCHIVES, NATIONAL GALLERY OF ART

SUPERIOR

Queen Anne mahogany drake-foot highboy, Philadelphia, circa 1750–1770. A choice example of excellent proportions. The arrangement of five rows of drawers in the upper case adds lift to the design. The stockinged drake feet and c-scrolled marginal carvings are rare refinements.

Ht: 71½" Wd: 43½" Dp: 22⅞"
Israel Sack, Inc.

MASTERPIECE

Queen Anne mahogany bonnet-top highboy, Townsend-Goddard group, Newport, Rhode Island, circa 1740–1760. The preference of the colonists for design with compact vertical emphasis was never more apparent than in this gem, especially in comparison to its New York cousin. This example's beauty is enhanced by a beautiful golden color and an untouched original surface. The carved shell and graceful cabriole legs conform in excellence.

Ht: 81½″ Wd: 38½″ Dp: 20½″   Private collection

BETTER

Queen Anne mahogany bonnet-top highboy with center pendant drop, Rhode Island, circa 1745–1765. This highboy has several design flaws. The stiff cabriole legs do not have desirable lift and the apron arch does not equal the high rise of the apron arch of the SUPERIOR example. The graduation is too abrupt between the upper and lower case making the lower case appear overly broad. The bonnet is somewhat flat and the small drawer inserted in the scrollboard does not integrate well into the design.

Ht: 82" Wd: 40½"

© 1977, SOTHEBY'S, INC.

SUPERIOR

Queen Anne mahogany bonnet-top highboy with center pendant drop, Newport, Rhode Island, circa 1745–1765. Only a handful of Queen Anne bonnet-top Newport highboys exist. It is fortunate to find one of such beautiful proportions and verticality. The graceful squared cabriole legs with slipper feet combine with a high-arched apron to effect a beautiful silhouette. The divided panels of the scrollboard are typical of the finer Newport products and serve to integrate the design. The beauty of this highboy is enhanced by a fine, nut-brown patina. Its value is many times that of lesser examples of this form.

Ht: 88" Wd: 39¼" Dp: 21½"
Historic Deerfield, Inc., Deerfield, Massachusetts

SUPERIOR

Queen Anne walnut bonnet-top slipper-foot highboy with center shell in the apron, Oyster Bay, Long Island, circa 1740–1770. The difficulty in grading is evident when considering this highly important document. In comparison with the Newport masterpiece, this piece presents a remarkable study of an identical form conditioned by the style preferences of two different regional centers. New York was more influenced by English horizontal emphasis and, like England, never really accepted the highboy as a preferred form. Thus, the broad proportion and the shorter legs are more suggestive of a chest-on-chest.

Ht: 84" Wd: 42½" Dp: 21½"
Society for the Preservation of Long Island Antiquities

BETTER

Q**ueen Anne mahogany bonnet-top highboy, Boston, circa 1740–1770.** The nicely formed cabriole legs, with c-scrolled marginal borders and fine bonnet top, do not prevent this highboy from being broad-based and somewhat heavy in proportion.

Ht: 87" Wd: 41" Dp: 21½"
(whereabouts unknown)

MASTERPIECE

Q**ueen Anne mahogany bonnet-top highboy, Boston or Newport, Rhode Island, circa 1740–1760.** The comparison between this majestic composition and its related counterpart demonstrates the importance of mastery of form. The vertical proportion is emphasized by the lift of the finely modeled cabriole leg, the narrowness of the case, and the high rise of the arch. The overhanging mid-molding and bat wing brasses are evidence of an early date in the Queen Anne era. The interior linings are red cedar. The beauty is enhanced by a magnificent bronze patina of great depth and mellowness. This highboy was brought to Nova Scotia during the time of the Revolutionary War and descended there until a generation ago.

Ht: 88½" Wd: 39½" Dp: 22¼"
Private collection
PHOTOGRAPH: ISRAEL SACK, INC.

BETTER

Queen Anne walnut bonnet-top high-boy, Massachusetts, circa 1740–1770. This otherwise fine highboy has three design defects: the plain two-drawer lower case is not as effective as the usual lower row of three divided drawers; the apron lacks a pleasing outline; and the cabriole legs are somewhat stiff.

Whereabouts unknown

PHOTOGRAPHIC ARCHIVES, NATIONAL GALLERY OF ART

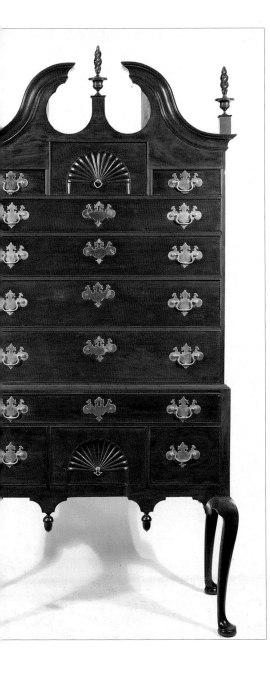

MASTERPIECE

Queen Anne mahogany bonnet-top highboy with fan-carved drawers, Massachusetts, circa 1750–1770. The mastery of proportion, fine craftsmanship, and unity of design is emphasized by comparison with the BETTER example. The cabriole legs, which have a high knee and slender well-turned ankle, add lift to the design. The flattened apron arches have more definition. Finely arched bonnet and flame finials develop the vertical effect. The character of this outstanding highboy is enhanced by original brasses, finials, and patina. The discriminating collector chooses a highboy of this quality, even if it is several times the price of a lesser competitor. It is fascinating to realize that the bonnet-top highboy is unique to the colonies. For all the thousands fashioned here, not one prototype has surfaced in England. It undoubtedly became popular in America because of our love of verticality and grace while the English preferred the chest-on-chest as more utilitarian.

Ht: 84¼" Wd: 40" Dp: 29½"
Private collection

BETTER

Chippendale cherry scroll-top highboy, Pennsylvania or Maryland, circa 1770–1785. What could be rarer than eagle-carved knees and inlaid initials? Rarity only becomes the dominant factor when the form and the quality are equal. In this instance, the case is supported on short, thick, dwarfish legs, the scroll opening is cramped, and the apron and shell carvings are not as refined as the MASTERPIECE example.

Ht: 94½" Wd: 44" Dp: 23"
Yale University Art Gallery
Mabel Brady Garvan Collection

MASTERPIECE

Chippendale mahogany scroll-top highboy, Philadelphia, circa 1770–1785. A master of the vertical proportion created this stately expression. The tall, finely modeled cabriole legs and rhythmic apron offer grace to what is often a massive or ponderous form. The figured grain serves to draw the composition together, and the high arch provides room for a spacious opening and beautiful scrollboard carving.

Ht: 99" Wd: 43¼" Dp: 22¾"   *Israel Sack, Inc.*

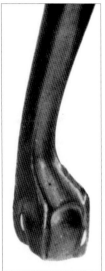

Detail of open claw foot.

BETTER

Chippendale mahogany bonnet-top highboy, open-taloned claw and ball feet, Rhode Island, circa 1760–1780. In the hands of an incompetent craftsman, even the rarest forms are of little interest to the connoisseur. Nothing is more sought after than examples of open taloned claw-and-ball-foot furniture of the Goddard-Townsend group. The ineptness of this model is brought into clear focus by comparison with its MASTERPIECE counterpart. The cabriole legs are stilted, the bonnet weak and the open-taloned claw and ball foot almost appears to be whittled rather than carved.

Whereabouts unknown

MASTERPIECE

Chippendale mahogany bonnet-top highboy with open-taloned claw and ball feet, Goddard-Townsend group, Newport, Rhode Island, circa 1760–1780. An outstanding example that makes the Newport bonnet-top highboy justly famous. Master craftsmanship is evident in the formation of the blocked bonnet, the effectiveness of the fluted quarter-columns, and the superb squared cabriole legs with sculptured open claw feet.

Ht: 81¼" Wd: 39" Dp: 20⅜"
Museum of Fine Arts, Boston
M. and M. Karolik Collection

tail of open
w foot.

BETTER

Chippendale walnut claw-and-ball-foot bonnet-top highboy with fan-carved drawers, Salem, Massachusetts, circa 1760–1780. This piece presents a startling comparison with the MASTERPIECE, as the pieces are the same basic form by makers of contrasting abilities. This piece lacks the same lift and grace, and the crest area appears cramped. The apron, which relates closely with that of the MASTERPIECE, is less skillfully wrought, particularly in the overly tight center volutes.

Ht: 88″ Wd: 41″   Whereabouts unknown

MASTERPIECE

Chippendale walnut claw-and-ball-foot bonnet-top highboy with wavy fan-carved drawers, Salem, Massachusetts, circa 1760–1780. This superb highboy combines the academic skill of the Boston school with the romantic flavor of the more free-spirited Salem school. The fans radiate in an alternating cyma pattern with a compensating scribed border. The spiral scrolled volutes centering the apron and the voluted knee returns add flourish to the cyma apron outline.

Ht: 88″ Wd: 42½″ Dp: 22¼″
Collection High Museum of Art, Atlanta;
purchased with funds from a supporter
of the Museum, 1976.1000.6

MASTERPIECE

Queen Anne cherry bonnet-top high-boy, Connecticut, circa 1770–1800. This diminutive symphony of grace and vibrancy was chosen to represent Connecticut Queen Anne achievement in the 1976 Bicentennial Yale–Victoria and Albert exhibition. The beautiful silhouette formed by the bandy legs and apron, the fine proportions, the convex shells serving as a fulcrum for the fans, and the pinwheel in the central plinth all place this piece on the highest level.

Ht: 86" Wd: 40" Dp: 18"
Collection of June and Joseph Hennage

BETTER

Queen Anne cherry bonnet-top high-boy, Connecticut, circa 1770–1800. Basically the same model as the MASTERPIECE, but what a world of difference there is. The cabriole legs do not have enough lift; the upper case has too much graduation, making the lower case appear heavy; and the large expanse of plain scrollboard and cramped arch opening spoil the fluency of this highboy.

Ht: 84" Wd: 39" Dp: 21½"
COURTESY OF CHRISTIE'S

BETTER

Chippendale mahogany scroll-top highboy with shell-and-vine-carved drawers, Philadelphia, circa 1760–1780 **(right).** The flattened arch, with the resulting cramped arch opening, and the somewhat short legs prevent this otherwise fine highboy from being a topnotch example.

Whereabouts unknown

PHOTOGRAPHIC ARCHIVES, NATIONAL GALLERY OF ART

BETTER-BEST

Chippendale mahogany scroll-top highboy with shell-and-vine-carved drawers, Philadelphia, possibly made by Thomas Affleck, circa 1760–1780 **(left).** This broadly proportioned highboy presents an amazing study in comparison to the MASTERPIECE. Its increased width offers more the feeling of a chest-on-chest than a highboy, and it must have been ordered especially with that capacious function in mind. A close comparison of the carving, apron, arch opening, rosettes, and finials makes it difficult to state that both were not from the same shop. The vertical proportion of the Hollingsworth highboy is far more satisfying.

Ht: 93" Wd: 47¼"

© 1977, SOTHEBY'S, INC.

MASTERPIECE

Chippendale walnut scroll-top highboy with shell-and-vine-carved drawers and cartouche ornament, made by Thomas Affleck for Levi Hollingsworth, Philadelphia, circa 1775–1780. While there are more elaborate and rococo, and probably more important, Philadelphia highboys, this piece excels in its vertical proportion and wonderful scale. The acanthus-carved legs have a desirable lift and unite with a rhythmic apron of tightly knit scrolls and lobes. The arch has a graceful curve and lift.

Ht: 94" Wd: 42" Dp: 20¾"   The Chipstone Foundation

PHOTOGRAPH: GAVIN ASHWORTH

LOWBOYS

BEST

William and Mary trumpet-leg lowboy with burl veneer, New York, circa 1710–1735. This rare lowboy is rated BEST even though it is of the broad proportion prevalent in New York case furniture. Pieces made employing burl veneer with herringbone borders evidenced the height of sophisticated technique used by master craftsmen of this period. The bell-shaped trumpet turnings are distinctively New York designs.

Whereabouts unknown

MASTERPIECE

William and Mary trumpet-leg lowboy with burl veneer, Massachusetts, circa 1710–1735. This piece is magnificent from every standpoint. The compact scale, the refinement of the turnings, and the exotic pattern of the burl veneer on the front and top are equaled by the superb proportions.

Ht: 30½" Wd: 33¼" Dp: 20¾"   *Private collection*

PHOTOGRAPH: ISRAEL SACK, INC.

BETTER

William and Mary cherry and maple trumpet-leg lowboy, inlaid date 1737, New York. The provincial character of this rare dated lowboy is apparent in the lack of skill in the turnings and stretchers, as well as in the breadth of the case. It is an important piece, but less refined in execution and in striking contrast to its Pennsylvania counterpart. The bell-shaped turning is typically New York.

Ht: 30" Wd: 34¾"   *Whereabouts unknown*

MASTERPIECE

William and Mary walnut trumpet-leg lowboy, inlaid date 1724, Philadelphia or Chester County, Pennsylvania. Not only are the compact proportions, choice turnings, rare center ball foot, and deep bronze patina exceptional, but the inlaid design is of rare beauty. The inlaid pattern, which is almost surrealistic, is highly competent, leading some experts to believe the lowboy to be of Philadelphia origin rather than from outside the city. The highly original and gifted artisan liked the finely turned ball feet so much he added a center foot to support the turned stretcher and finial. The drawer separation and the elliptical turnings are Pennsylvania features. The dated evidence that this masterpiece precedes its New York counterpart by thirteen years proves that refined elements do not always indicate a later date.

Ht: 30" Wd: 40¼" Dp: 23⅜"   *Philadelphia Museum of Art*

Detail of inlay.

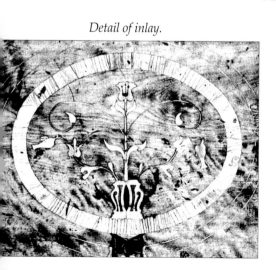

BETTER

Queen Anne cherry fan-carved lowboy with scribed pad feet, Connecticut, circa 1760–1780. The boxy case and the relatively short cabriole legs present an interesting comparison with the exciting lines and detail of the SUPERIOR example.

Whereabouts unknown

PHOTOGRAPHIC ARCHIVES, NATIONAL GALLERY OF ART

SUPERIOR

Queen Anne cherry fan-carved lowboy with scribed pad feet, Connecticut, circa 1760–1780. The Connecticut innovative spirit is expressed brilliantly in the fluted and scroll-carved legs and insteps. The lift of the design is aided by the dancing spurred feet and the graceful contours of the pointed arch apron.

Ht: 33" Wd: 35¾" Dp: 21¼"   Collection of Mr. and Mrs. Robert Youngen

ENGLISH

Queen Anne walnut lowboy, rural England, circa 1720–1750. The simplicity of this non-urban English lowboy more logically serves as a source influence for its American counterparts than the more elaborate London counterparts. The horizontal emphasis is typical of English domestic products.

Whereabouts unknown

PHOTOGRAPHIC ARCHIVES, NATIONAL GALLERY OF ART

AMERICAN: BETTER

Queen Anne walnut lowboy, Massachusetts, circa 1740–1770. The vertical emphasis, so typical of New England, is apparent. Although the cabriole legs and apron are well formed, the case is boxy, the façade below the drawers too deep, and the top slightly skimpy for the design.

Whereabouts unknown

AMERICAN: SUPERIOR

Queen Anne walnut lowboy with crotch walnut veneer, Massachusetts, circa 1735–1750. A compact gem of perfect proportions. The top is veneered in eight crotch-veneered sections instead of the usual four, bringing more excitement and complexity to its design. The spurred quarter-round knee returns and the smooth curve of the rounded knees add refined touches.

Ht: 29¾" Wd: 33¾" Dp: 21½"
Private collection

AMERICAN: MASTERPIECE

Queen Anne walnut block-front lowboy with crotch walnut veneer, Salem, Massachu-setts, circa 1735–1750. This magnificent, rare creation is the first crotch-veneered block-front piece to be discovered. The problem of integration is solved by having the arched outlines of the apron cut from the continuation of the blocking. The beauty of the complex formation is enhanced by the richly figured crotch veneer with its check-ered inlaid borders. The inlaid center shell projects forward, built out by a thick pine background. The smoothly curved cabriole legs and knee returns resemble those of the SUPERIOR lowboy. The top is veneered in quartered sections.

Ht: 30¼" Wd: 34¼" Dp: 21⅞"   *Collection of Mr. and Mrs. George M. Kaufman*

PHOTOGRAPH: ISRAEL SACK, INC.

BETTER

Queen Anne cherry lowboy with fan-carved apron, Connecticut, circa 1750–1770. A nice rural piece with great aspect. However, the cabriole legs are relatively stiff and thick, and the apron fan is crudely formed. Although not comparable in value to the other examples in this comparison, it has a country charm, enhanced by an undisturbed original surface.

Ht: 30" Wd: 36" Dp: 22½"
Whereabouts unknown

BEST

Queen Anne mahogany lowboy with fan-carved apron, Rhode Island or Connecticut, circa 1750–1770. A finely modeled example by an urban master craftsman. Note the choice mahogany, the smooth curve of the cabriole legs, the nicely scrolled apron, and the well-defined shell.

Ht: 29½" Wd: 33" Dp: 19½"
Dr. and Mrs. Clifford A. Poppens

SUPERIOR

Queen Anne mahogany lowboy with fan-carved center drawer, Connecticut or Salem, Massachusetts, circa 1750–1770. A choice example by a highly skilled designer and craftsman. The deep fan-carved center drawer is extended into a concave blocked apron with a cupid's bow outline, creating a dynamic effect. The cabriole legs are boldly curved.

Ht: 31½" Wd: 34½" Dp: 22½"
Private collection

Profile view.

Detail of leg.

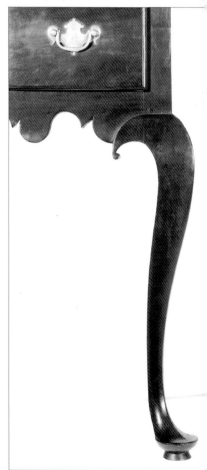

MASTERPIECE

Queen Anne mahogany lowboy with fan-carved center drawer, Salem, Massachusetts, circa 1750–1770. If one case piece were chosen to represent the creative genius of American Queen Anne design, this could well be the one. It achieves in excitement of form what the greatest English masterpieces achieve in carving. It combines the daring vibrancy and restlessness, more often seen in rural interpretations, with the skill of a master. The excitement of the powerfully wrought undulating apron curves is continued to the dramatically voluted knee returns. The boldly curved cabriole legs fashioned from the square serve to emphasize the outline and end in crisp wafer pad platformed feet (see detail). The cutout diamond center and the scrolled voluted knee brackets with ridged top surface are Salem features, as is the sharp curve of the ankle as it turns into the pad foot.

Ht: 30¾" Wd: 35" Dp: 22½"   The Art Institute of Chicago
Gift of the Antiquarian Society through William O. Hunt, Jessie Spalding Landon, Mrs. Harold T. Martin, Adelaide Ryerson, and Alex Vance Funds.
PHOTOGRAPH: ISRAEL SACK, INC.

BETTER

Queen Anne cherry lowboy with floral carved center drawer, Connecticut, circa 1760–1780. The small center drawer seems somewhat crushed by the wide drawers flanking it and the cabriole legs are slightly stiff. A nice feature, however, is the retaining molding which unites the top with the case.

Whereabouts unknown
PHOTOGRAPHIC ARCHIVES, NATIONAL GALLERY OF ART

SUPERIOR

Queen Anne cherry lowboy with spiral fan-carved drawer, Connecticut, circa 1760–1780. This lowboy is worth several times more than the BETTER example; the gracefulness of the well-formed cabriole legs is obvious when comparing this SUPERIOR example. The carved pinwheel in the lower center drawer is uncrowded and integrates successfully into the overall composition.

Ht: 32¾″ Wd: 34″ Dp: 21″
Private collection

BETTER

Queen Anne cherry scalloped-top lowboy, Connecticut, circa 1750–1780. The beautiful scalloped top seems wasted on the simple case with its bland drawer arrangement. The apron design is successful, but the knees of the cabriole legs swell too far down, losing the grace that is evident in the SUPERIOR example.

Whereabouts unknown

SUPERIOR

Queen Anne cherry scalloped-top lowboy, Connecticut, circa 1750–1780. This piece is a study in symmetry achieved in a daring composition. The contained restless movement of the cyma-curved top is successfully balanced by a well-formed case with central fan and a beautiful silhouette formed by bandy curved legs and a nicely scrolled apron.

Formerly Israel Sack, Inc.
(whereabouts unknown)

BETTER

Queen Anne mahogany slipper-foot lowboy, Newport, Rhode Island, circa 1740–1760. A beautiful cyma-scrolled apron does not overcome the lack of bend of the cabriole leg and the anemic flow of the ankle and slipper foot.

© SOTHEBY'S, INC.

SUPERIOR

Queen Anne mahogany slipper-foot lowboy, Newport, Rhode Island, circa 1740–1760. The graceful outline developed to a high degree by the Goddard-Townsend master craftsmen is evident in this piece. Note the sharp delineation of the ridged cabriole legs.

Ht: 32" Wd: 36" Dp: 21½"   *Israel Sack, Inc.*

MASTERPIECE

Queen Anne mahogany slipper-foot lowboy, Newport, Rhode Island, circa 1740–1760. Consummate grace is achieved by the artful thinning of the squared cabriole legs into a sinuous outline centered by a deeply carved Goddard-Townsend shell. The beauty is enhanced by an original bronze patina.

Ht: 30¾" Wd: 34¼" Dp: 22½"
Collection of Yvette and Tom Cole
PHOTOGRAPH: ISRAEL SACK, INC.

BETTER

Queen Anne walnut or mahogany drake-foot lowboy, Philadelphia, circa 1750–1770. The designer of this lowboy crowded its fishtail apron, which is identical to that of the MASTERPIECE, into too narrow a space. The result is that the apron droops and the case has a boxy appearance.

Whereabouts unknown

SUPERIOR-MASTERPIECE

Queen Anne mahogany drake-foot lowboy, Philadelphia, circa 1750–1770. A finely sculpted model of beautiful design and flawless execution. The high arch with fishtail center effectively lightens the composition. The scrolled voluted knee returns, the softening of the case by the chamfered fluted corners, and the beautifully scrolled side apron add to the stature of this fine creation.

Ht: 29¼″ Wd: 34″ Dp: 20¼″   Private collection

Detail of side.

Detail of leg.

MASTERPIECE

Queen Anne mahogany drake-foot lowboy with shell-and-vine-carved center drawer, Philadelphia, circa 1750–1770. The ultimate in a Queen Anne Philadelphia lowboy. It excels in proportion, refinement of detail, and integrated design. The leg detail shows the five-lobed stockinged drake foot with a cyma outline of its own. The scrolled volutes blend with the apron outline. A retaining molding under the overhanging top unites it with the case. The original condition of the piece and the crispness of its outline are as appealing as the design itself. An identical example has lost its applied vines, but they "grew back" later.

Ht: 29¾" Wd: 33¾" Dp: 21¼"   *Private collection*

PHOTOGRAPH: ISRAEL SACK, INC.

GOOD

Queen Anne drake-foot lowboy, Pennsylvania, circa 1740–1760. The squat, angular legs, the lack of lift of the apron, and the excessive overhang of the top make this model unsuccessful.

Whereabouts unknown

BETTER

Queen Anne walnut drake-foot lowboy, Pennsylvania, probably Philadelphia, circa 1740–1760. This lowboy shows the hand of a competent craftsman, but the case is somewhat broad.

Ht: 30" Wd: 35½" Dp: 20½"
Whereabouts unknown

SUPERIOR

Queen Anne drake-foot lowboy, Philadelphia, circa 1745–1770. This is a compact example, with fine scrolled and spurred apron, squared cabriole legs which end in stockinged drake feet, and fluted chamfered corners which soften the case outline. All these are features that outshine the standard model.

Ht: 30" Wd: 34" Dp: 20½"
Formerly Israel Sack, Inc.
(whereabouts unknown)

MASTERPIECE

Queen Anne drake-foot lowboy, Philadelphia and vicinity, circa 1750–1770. A superb model that shows the heights a gifted artisan can reach working in the conventional mold. The case is compact, the chamfered fluted corners soften the outline, the top drawer simulates three drawers, helping to draw the composition together. The apron has a beautiful outline, adding lift to the design, assisted by the gracefully modeled cabriole legs. Although a good number of drake-foot lowboys have survived, few of these reach this level of development and beauty.

Ht: 30⅜" Wd: 35" Dp: 21¾"   Private collection

BETTER

Queen Anne curly maple Spanish-foot lowboy, Delaware Valley, circa 1750–1770. The stiff, short, squared legs of this lowboy are a startling contrast to the successful curves of the almost identical MASTERPIECE example.

Ht: 28¾" Wd: 39¼" Dp: 22¾"

© 1988, SOTHEBY'S, INC.

MASTERPIECE

Queen Anne curly maple Spanish-foot lowboy, Delaware Valley, circa 1750–1770. A beautiful example with gracefully curved cabriole legs resulting in a successful and romantic composition. The finely modeled squared cabriole legs add lift to the design. The combination of squared cabriole legs and cuffed Spanish feet is typical of work from the Delaware Valley. This lowboy was in the landmark Howard Reifsnyder sale in 1929.

Ht: 29¼" Wd: 32½" Dp: 20"

COURTESY OF CHRISTIE'S

BETTER

Chippendale walnut claw-and-ball-foot lowboy with shell-and-vine-carved center drawer, Philadelphia, circa 1760–1780. A fine example, with exceptional cyma-shaped top corners. The piece suffers a bit because of its short cabriole legs and a lack of crispness to the claw and ball feet.

Whereabouts unknown

SUPERIOR

Chippendale walnut claw-and-ball-foot lowboy with shell-and-vine-carved center drawer, Philadelphia, circa 1760–1780. The taller, nicely curved cabriole legs effect a finer proportion than the BETTER example. Also, the talons of the claw and ball feet are more definitive.

Ht: 29" Wd: 34" Dp: 21½"
Private collection

MASTERPIECE

Chippendale walnut claw-and-ball-foot lowboy with shell-and-vine carved center drawer made by Thomas Affleck for Levi Hollingsworth, Philadelphia, circa 1760–1770 (companion to the matching highboy on page 201). Few Philadelphia lowboys succeed in proportion and integrated design as well as this example does. The depth of the case is in perfect ratio to the height of the finely modeled, acanthus-carved cabriole legs. The legs unite rhythmically with the scrolled apron, and a graceful silhouette develops. Mastery of form and understated elegance serve to place this lowboy on a par or superior to more ambitious but less balanced pieces.

Ht: 30½" Wd: 33¾" Dp: 19¾"
The Chipstone Foundation
PHOTOGRAPH: GAVIN ASHWORTH

BETTER

Chippendale maple claw-and-ball-foot lowboy, Salem, Massachusetts, or vicinity, circa 1760–1780. This is the same general form as its SUPERIOR comparison but with a world of difference. The case is relatively boxy or squarish, the apron outline is somewhat provincial in execution, and the curve of the cabriole leg is less fluent. For the form to be made in maple is quite rare; the use of this primary native wood suggests its origin in a smaller town away from the more urban centers.

Whereabouts unknown

BETTER

Chippendale mahogany claw-and-ball-foot lowboy with shell-carved center drawer, Philadelphia, circa 1760–1780. The overly deep top drawer and the short cabriole legs give a heavy, boxy look to this example. It once could have had carved vines flanking the shell on the drawer and an applied shell in the center of the apron.

Whereabouts unknown

PHOTOGRAPHIC ARCHIVES, NATIONAL GALLERY OF ART

SUPERIOR

Chippendale mahogany claw-and-ball-foot lowboy, Salem, Massachusetts, circa 1760–1780. This outstanding example is of balanced proportion with a compact case, beautifully scrolled apron, a dramatic, finely carved central fan, and well-modeled cabriole legs with voluted knee brackets.

Private collection

MASTERPIECE

Chippendale curly maple claw-and-ball-foot lowboy with shell-and-vine-carved center drawer, Philadelphia, circa 1760–1780. This lowboy would rate as an outstanding Philadelphia lowboy if it was made in the more typical medium of walnut or mahogany. In curly maple it is supreme. The case is gracefully supported on well-modeled cabriole legs and an apron formed of c-scrolls and volutes, centered by a webbed shell.

Ht: 32" Wd: 34" Dp: 20⅝"
Private collection

BEST

Chippendale walnut claw-and-ball-foot lowboy, Philadelphia, circa 1760–1780. This fine example has fluted quarter-columns, scrolled and voluted knee returns, a molding which unites the top with the case, and a nicely scrolled apron—all the refinements of a top-quality unadorned lowboy. It suffers only by comparison to the MASTERPIECE example.

Ht: 29¼" Wd: 35½" Dp: 21"
Whereabouts unknown

MASTERPIECE

Chippendale walnut claw-and-ball-foot lowboy, Philadelphia, circa 1760–1780. By compressing the case into a compact framework, this artisan created a masterpiece from an otherwise conventional form. The modeling, the choice of figured grain, and the magnificent golden color it has attained add to its rare beauty. Many connoisseurs would choose this piece over its more richly carved peers.

Ht: 29½" Wd: 34¾" Dp: 21½"   *Private collection*
PHOTOGRAPH: ISRAEL SACK, INC.

BETTER

Chippendale walnut claw-and-ball-foot-carved lowboy, Lancaster, Pennsylvania, circa 1770–1785. In their own fiercely independent way, the rural craftsmen of Lancaster emulated the master craftsmen of Philadelphia. The carving is almost surrealistic, and with its stippled background, it dominates the form. The resulting lowboy, though dramatic, is heavy.

COURTESY OF CHRISTIE'S

MASTERPIECE

Chippendale mahogany claw-and-ball-foot-carved lowboy, Philadelphia, circa 1765–1780. One of the supreme achievements by a master craftsman of Philadelphia. The magnificence of the carving blends with a superbly integrated form. As was often the case in Philadelphia, a master carver may have collaborated with a master cabinetmaker to produce this creation. One's eye can focus only on the united composition.

Private collection
PHOTOGRAPH: ISRAEL SACK, INC.

Detail of carving.

MIRRORS

BEST

William and Mary walnut mirror with cutout design, American or English, **circa 1690–1720.** A very scarce form. The removable crests rarely survive intact.

Ht: 23½" Wd: 12"   *Israel Sack, Inc.*

SUPERIOR

William and Mary mirror, walnut veneer on pine, removable crest with cutout design, original engraved glass, American or English, circa 1710–1730. This is a higher order of early mirrors with the engraved top glass, ogival molded mirror border, and superior proportions.

Ht: 37½" Wd: 16½"   *Private collection*

BETTER

Chippendale mahogany mirror with scrolled crest and base, American or English, circa 1760–1780. The scrolling is heavy and crowded. The squared proportion is not as desirable for American taste as the proportion of the SUPERIOR mirror.

© 1988, SOTHEBY'S, INC.

SUPERIOR

Chippendale mahogany mirror with scrolled crest and base, probably American, possibly English, circa 1760–1780. Whether American or English, this mirror definitely reflects the New England taste in its proportion and finesse in scrolling. The edges of the scrolling are slightly beveled to create a sharper outline.

Private collection

SUPERIOR- MASTERPIECE

Hepplewhite mahogany and gilt mirror in Chippendale form, inscribed *Luther Woodbury*, Beverly, Massachusetts, circa 1780–1800. This beautiful mirror is important as a document, since it proves that at least one scrolled mirror was made in this country. The script below reads, *"30 leaves, 12 horns"* denoting the quantity of gilt employed.

Ht: 43" Wd: 23½"   *Private collection*

MASTERPIECE

Queen Anne walnut mirror with pierced shell and carved, gilded side leaves, American or English, circa 1750–1760 (below). The strapwork scrolling of the ears and the carved and gilded side leaves contribute to make this one of the finest Queen Anne mirrors in the colonies, whether it was made here or imported.

Ht: 59½" Wd: 20½"   *Israel Sack, Inc.*

SUPERIOR

Queen Anne walnut mirror with pierced shell, American or English, circa 1750–1760 (above). The fine scroll of the crest suggests the emerging Chippendale influence. The two-section glasses are bordered by bold ogival segmented molding typical of this form of mirror.

Formerly collection of Charles K. Davis (whereabouts unknown)

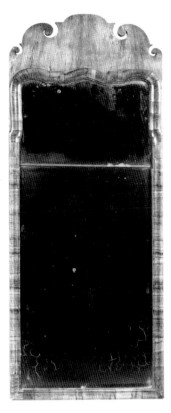

BEST

Queen Anne mirror with beveled two-section glass, American or English, circa 1730–1750 (above). Any mirror of this period that survives intact with the original two-section glasses and the ogival molded mirror borders is highly desirable and rare. The simple scrolling of the crest precedes in date those mirrors with more refined scrolling.

Ht: 44" Wd: 18"   Israel Sack, Inc.

MASTERPIECE

Queen Anne walnut mirror with beveled two-section glass, engraved top glass, American or English, circa 1730–1750 (right). One of the finest of this group of early Queen Anne mirrors. It retains the old or original grained surface. The beveling of the top glass follows the outline of the ogival border.

Ht: 61" Wd: 19"   Israel Sack, Inc.

BETTER

Late Chippendale mahogany scrolled mirror with gilded phoenix in crest, American, circa 1780–1800 (left). The scrolling, though competent, does not have the delicacy of the BEST example, and the gilt phoenix is not as skillfully sculptured. The line inlaid mirror border gives credence to its American origin.

Ht: 43½″ Wd: 23½″   Israel Sack, Inc.

BEST

Chippendale mahogany scrolled mirror with gilded phoenix in crest, American or English, circa 1760–1780 (right). This is a competent small example with slender proportions, nicely voluted ears, and a well-modeled phoenix.

Ht: 26½″ Wd: 14¾″   Israel Sack, Inc.

MASTERPIECE

Pair of Chippendale mahogany scrolled mirrors with facing gilded phoenixes and scrolled vines, Massachusetts or English, circa 1760–1780. This beautiful form of scrolled mirror with vine tracery seems to turn up only in Massachusetts, lending credence to the possibility that some were made here. In any event, they are one of the most artistic forms of Chippendale mirrors. The existence of a matching pair is remarkable.

Ht: 40½″ Wd: 22¾″   Private collection

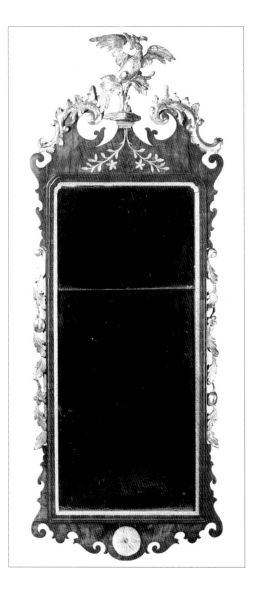

MASTERPIECE

Chippendale mahogany and gilt pier mirror with phoenix ornament and side leaves, New York or English, circa 1760–1780 (left). To me, this is one of the most beautiful Chippendale mirrors, whether made in the colonies or in the mother country. We do know it was made for the Ten Eyck family of Albany and remained in that family since the Revolution. It excels in the vertical proportion, the magnificent sculpturing of the leaves, cornice, and ornament, and in the integration of the elements.

Ht: 64" Wd: 24½"   Private collection

PHOTOGRAPH: ISRAEL SACK, INC.

MASTERPIECE

Chippendale crotch walnut and gilt "Constitution" mirror with eagle ornament, American or English, circa 1760–1775 (right). A superb example, distinguished by its finely sculptured eagle and original patina and gilt. The slender proportion epitomizes the preference of the colonists for the vertical emphasis.

Ht: 62" Wd: 29½"   Private collection

BEST

Hepplewhite mahogany and gilt mirror with urn ornament and side leaves, New York, circa 1780–1800. This is the first major form of mirror that can definitely be ascribed to New York and, as far as we know, has no English prototype. A considerable number were made here after the Revolution, but few survive intact with the original side leaves and ornament.

Ht: 53″ Wd: 21″
Formerly Israel Sack, Inc.
(whereabouts unknown)

SUPERIOR

Hepplewhite mahogany and gilt mirror with urn ornament and side leaves, New York, circa 1780–1800 (left). This is a very choice example with a graceful arched crest, a beautiful shell patera in the scrollboard, and finely outlined scrollwork. The wheat and floral stalks are artistically arranged.

Ht: 58″ Wd: 22¾″   *Private collection*

MASTERPIECE

Hepplewhite mahogany and gilt mirror with eagle inlay, urn ornament, side leaves, and eglomise panel, New York, circa 1780–1800 (right). One of the finest of all New York Hepplewhite mirrors. It excels in its vertical proportion, its beautiful eglomise panel, the artistic urn and floral side leaves, as well as the eagle-inlaid patera, depicting the symbol of our new Republic.

Ht: 66½″ Wd: 24¼″   *Private collection*

BETTER

S heraton gilded mirror, eglomise panel depicting the three graces, labeled *Cermenati and Mon Frino, Boston,* **circa 1800–1815.** Despite the label, neither the quality of the frame or the painting measure up to that of the SUPERIOR mirror. The frame is squarish and lacks the overhanging cornice.

Whereabouts unknown

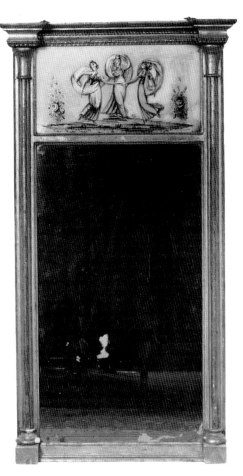

SUPERIOR

S heraton gilded mirror, eglomise panel depicting the three graces, Boston, circa 1800–1815. This mirror shows architectural balance and an eglomise painting by a fine Boston artist. The cylindrical columns are sanded and gilded, a feature seen on Gilbert Stuart portrait frames but rare and effective on a mirror of this form. The original gilt has lost none of its brilliance.

Ht: 35¼″ Wd: 19¼″   Private collection

GOOD-BETTER

Sheraton rectangular gilt mirror with eglomise glass panels and eagle ornament, New York, circa 1810–1825. A less-than-desirable example of a group of important New York mirrors. This was rather harshly described in *Fine Points I* as a "clumsy mirror with clumsy eagle." Actually, the eagle is not too inept and the eglomise scene is pleasing, but the overall effect is heavy and uncoordinated.

Whereabouts unknown

MASTERPIECE

Sheraton rectangular gilt mirror with eglomise glass panel depicting New York from Brooklyn Heights, eagle center ornament with eglomise center and end panels, and drapery chains, New York, circa 1800–1815. There is so much that can go wrong with any of these mirrors that it is a miracle one like this would survive intact. The scenic panel with additional eglomise center plinth and triangular end plinths are beautifully designed and painted. The quality of the sculptured modeled and gilded eagle is repeated in the molded elements of the frame. This is one of the supreme mirrors of this group, and it is in superb original condition.

Collection of Eric Noah

BEST

Sheraton gilt overmantle mirror, labeled by Thomas Natt, Philadelphia, circa 1800–1820. One of the very few, labeled American overmantle mirrors. It has an interesting frieze of diagonal and floral repeats but lacks the more interesting eglomise panels on the more developed examples

Ht: 28¾" Wd: 44¾"   *Private collection*

MASTERPIECE

Sheraton gilt overmantle mirror with eglomise glass panels, New York, circa 1800–1815. The effectiveness of the central oval mirror panel, flanked by gilt, carved spandrels, combines with the eglomise-paneled frieze to create a beautiful composition.

Ht: 36" Wd: 59½"   *Private collection*

BETTER

Sheraton gilt mirror, eglomise panel depicting tomb of Washington and American flags, Boston, circa 1800–1815. Patriotic emblems eulogizing Washington and the new Republic were favorite themes of early nineteenth-century artists. This proud depiction is contained in a frame of average quality.

Metropolitan Museum of Art; gift of Mrs. Russell Sage, 1909

SUPERIOR

Sheraton gilt mirror, eglomise panel depicting tomb of Washington, American flags, and allegoric female figures of Hope and Plenty, labeled by B. Cermenati and Co., Boston, circa 1805–1815. The Boston label preserved on a mirror of this outstanding quality enhances the value. If the label were on the BETTER mirror and this mirror were unlabeled, this would still be more valuable. It proves the principle that labels, documentation, and history become relevant only when the object itself reaches the art status.

Ht: 64½" Wd: 30"   Private collection

BETTER

Classical gilt convex mirror with eagle ornament, American or English, circa 1810–1825 (left). The frame is relatively heavy and the ornamentation is crowded. The design lacks the grace and verticality of its companions.

Whereabouts unknown

SUPERIOR

Classical gilt convex mirror with black eagle ornament, attributed to John Doggett, Boston, circa 1800–1815 (right). It is often difficult to distinguish the origin of convex mirrors between England and the colonies. Though not labeled, the relationship of the design elements to the engraved Doggett label points to the probability of Boston origin for this fine mirror. John Doggett was Boston's leading mirror maker.

Ht: 53″ Wd: 29″   Private collection

Detail of label. Note the similarity of the intertwining dolphins and the pointed leaves of the plinth supporting the eagle.

MASTERPIECE

Classical gilt convex mirror with eagle ornament, Boston or Salem, Massachusetts, circa 1800–1815. This superb work of art combines exquisite delicacy, balance, and sculptural perfection. The eagle seems poised in preparation for flight and holds in his beak a drapery of chains with tassels. The carved drapery base relates to the work of Salem carvers and the candle brackets have cut-glass candle holders.

Ht: 52″ Wd: 24½″
Collection of Mr. and Mrs. Eddy G. Nicholson
PHOTOGRAPH: ISRAEL SACK, INC.

SIDEBOARDS

BETTER

Hepplewhite mahogany small inlaid sideboard, straight front with ovolu ends, Massachusetts, circa 1780–1800 (descended from Revolutionary General John Stark). The only criticism of this rare small sideboard is the mass of the arched area below the center drawer. Comparison with the BEST example demonstrates the effectiveness of subtle design improvements.

Ht: 41" Wd: 59" Dp: 22¾"
Whereabouts unknown

PHOTOGRAPH: ISRAEL SACK, INC.

BEST

Hepplewhite mahogany small inlaid sideboard, straight front with ovolu ends, Massachusetts, circa 1780–1800. The oval panel on the center drawer and the lifting of the arched apron creates a lighter effect on a similar form.

Ht: 40½" Wd: 67" Dp: 27"

© 1988, SOTHEBY'S, INC.

MASTERPIECE

Hepplewhite mahogany inlaid bow-front sideboard, Maryland, circa 1780–1800. The rare small size, the vase and floral inlaid stiles, and the exquisite delicate proportions make this creation a collector's dream.

Ht: 30½" Wd: 47¾" Dp: 18¾"   *Collection of Mr. and Mrs. Lawrence Fleischman*

BETTER

Hepplewhite mahogany inlaid serpentine-front sideboard with marble top, Massachusetts, circa 1780–1800. The rarity of the marble top does not keep this sideboard from being ponderous. The deep case and the top row of drawers are out of proportion to the inlaid short legs.

Ht: 40½" Wd: 66" Dp: 28½"

© 1988, SOTHEBY'S, INC.

BETTER

Hepplewhite mahogany serpentine-front sideboard, Rhode Island, circa 1780–1800. While the case is slightly heavy, the ratio of the case to the leg height is greatly improved. The richly figured veneer of the cabinet doors does not fully eliminate the feeling of mass.

Whereabouts unknown

PHOTOGRAPH: JOHN HOPF

SUPERIOR

Hepplewhite mahogany inlaid serpentine-front sideboard, New York, circa 1780–1800. Several features make this sideboard outstanding: the perfect ratio of case to legs; the canted center legs, which have a knife blade effect when viewed from the front and serve to smooth the flow of the concave and convex curves; the oval and circular panels of dark and light inlay that effectively eliminate any feeling of mass. The perfection of form would make this sideboard more desirable and valuable than a more highly inlaid sideboard of less perfect proportions.

Ht: 40" Wd: 72½" Dp: 26¾"
Collection of Mr. and
Mrs. William C. Buck

MASTERPIECE

Hepplewhite mahogany inlaid serpentine-front sideboard with matching knife boxes, labeled by William Whitehead, New York, circa 1780–1800. This would be one of the supreme American sideboards without the documentation but as a labeled example, it is priceless. The exquisite proportions, the inlaid patterns which blend into the design, the original finish and brasses, and the rare companion knife boxes combine to make this a chef d'oeuvre. The canted center legs serve to allow an uninterrupted flow of the ends with the bowed recessed cupboard, which in turn serves to lighten the weight of the bowed row of drawers above.

Ht: 40" Wd: 72"
Collection High Museum of Art, Atlanta;
purchase with funds from a supporter
of the museum, 1976.1000.5
PHOTOGRAPH: ISRAEL SACK, INC.

Detail: The bellflower inlay, connected by loops with pellet drops, is distinctive of the work of William Whitehead. Similar looped bellflower inlay appears in some Baltimore pieces.

BEST

Hepplewhite mahogany inlaid straight-front sideboard with recessed cupboard, New York, circa 1780–1800. This sideboard represents top quality for its form. There is no doubt, however, that the serpentine-front interpretations are more beautiful, and consequently more valuable.

Ht: 39½" Wd: 70"

© 1945, SOTHEBY'S, INC.

SUPERIOR

Hepplewhite mahogany inlaid sideboard with serpentine center, bowed ends, and recessed cupboard, New York, circa 1780–1800. The beautiful contours of this sideboard represent a group of highly successful New York sideboards of similar form.

Ht: 41½" Wd: 76¼" Dp: 27"
Collection of Mr. and Mrs. Robert J. Hurst

MASTERPIECE

Hepplewhite mahogany inlaid serpentine-front sideboard with recessed cupboard, labeled by William Whitehead, New York, circa 1780–1800. This beautiful example of a popular New York form establishes William Whitehead as perhaps the most gifted cabinet-maker and designer of the New York Hepplewhite era. The distinctive leg inlay of delicate bellflower and pellet inlay connected by loops has become Whitehead's trademark. The choice of superb crotch-figured veneer contained in oval and circular double-line inlaid borders creates a flowing continuity within the body of the board. The full labels on this sideboard establish the partially missing labels on the High Museum MASTERPIECE.

Ht: 40" Wd: 72" Dp: 29½"
Private collection

BEST

Hepplewhite mahogany bellflower-inlaid, bow-front small sideboard, Massachusetts, circa 1780–1800. This pleasing sideboard is of a rare small size. The cupboard door shows fine crotch grain rising vertically. The top edge is a simple strip of birch rather than cross-banded.

Formerly Israel Sack, Inc.
(whereabouts unknown)

MASTERPIECE

Hepplewhite mahogany floral-and-fan-inlaid, bow-front small sideboard, Massachusetts, circa 1780–1800. This model begins where the BEST example leaves off. The doors and drawers are bordered by curly maple cross-banding, while the doors have dark and light fan quadrants in the corners. The star and floral inlay on the legs and stiles and the cross-banded edge of the top border add to the beauty of this piece. It is a brilliant creation with a golden patina.

Ht: 39⅜" Wd: 54" Dp: 22"   *Collection of June and Joseph Hennage*

BEST

Sheraton mahogany inlaid sideboard with reeded turret columns, bulbous reeded legs, Boston, circa 1800–1815. A fine-quality sideboard made by a first-rate Boston craftsman. A tendency toward massive proportions inherent in a rectangular case is avoided by the careful choice of fine veneer and cross-banding and the successful ratio of case to well-formed reeded legs.

Ht: 41½" Wd: 74"   *Whereabouts unknown*

Detail: The superb detail of the tambour shutters, inlaid borders, carved elements, and ivory escutcheons rivals any masterworks of contemporary England, yet blends into the overall composition.

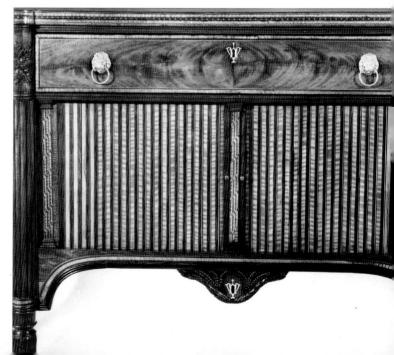

MASTERPIECE

Sheraton mahogany inlaid sideboard with reeded turrets, satinwood and mahogany tambours, made by John Seymour and Son, carving attributed to Thomas Whitman, Boston, circa 1800–1810 (above, and detail at left). One of the most important American sideboards, this bears a close relationship to the Andrew Varick Stout example in the Metropolitan Museum. It is interesting to see how the master designer and genius artisan transformed the basic form of the previous example into a supreme achievement.

Ht: 40½" Wd: 73½" Dp: 26½"   Private collection

PHOTOGRAPH: ISRAEL SACK, INC.

SUPERIOR

Hepplewhite walnut and birch veneer, serpentine-front sideboard with tiered gallery, Augusta, Georgia, circa 1780–1800. The successful integrating of the rare gallery with the case is accomplished by careful placement of oval, rectangular, and circular panels. The borders of the apron, top edge, and gallery are highlighted by rosewood light and dark cross-banded veneer. Even though this piece represents an earlier period than its Charleston counterpart, the two could easily have been made about the same date.

Ht: 46⅛″ Wd: 72⅝″ Dp: 30½″
Collection of the Museum of Early Southern Decorative Arts, #2105

MASTERPIECE

Sheraton mahogany inlaid sideboard with concave tambour center and ovolu ends with attached gallery, Charlestown, South Carolina, circa 1800–1810. The magnificence of this work of art defies description. How do you describe a beautiful sunset? The mystery of the scarcity of identifiable Charleston major works is deepened when one realizes that if this chef d'oeuvre exists there must be others not yet discovered. The inlaid center panels depict the cotton plant and buds. With all its mass, the piece seems light and well integrated.

Ht: 40½″, with gallery 57¼″ Wd: 89¾″ Dp: 30⅞″
Yale University Art Gallery, the Mabel Brady Garvan Collection

MASTERPIECE
example appears
on page 244.

BETTER

Sheraton mahogany sideboard with bowed center, Ephraim Haines school, Philadelphia, circa 1800–1815. The figured veneer is high quality. The legs, while uncarved and unreeded, are related to documented examples by Ephraim Haines. The contour of the bowed center with straight wings is not as fluent as the SUPERIOR example.

Ht: 41" Wd: 66" Dp: 24½"   *Whereabouts unknown*

SUPERIOR

Sheraton mahogany kidney-shaped sideboard, attributed to Ephraim Haines, Philadelphia, circa 1800–1815. The concave center of this fine sideboard alleviates its mass, effecting a lighter appearance. The legs have acanthus-carved capitals and tapered reeding. Both the distinctive capital carving and the disc turning of the feet are recognized as the work of Ephraim Haines.

Ht: 42" Wd: 73" Dp: 27"   *Private collection*

MASTERPIECE

Hepplewhite mahogany inlaid kidney-shaped sideboard, Baltimore, circa 1780–1800. The rare and desirable kidney shape of this sideboard is enhanced by beautiful inlaid ovals and circles set into finely figured mahogany veneered panels. The stiles are fronted by inlaid bellflowers supported by ram's heads in curly satinwood backgrounds. A rich brown patina adds to the excitement of this design and form created by a competent cabinetmaker.

Ht: 38" Wd: 70½" Dp: 25"   *Private collection*

SOFAS

BEST

Chippendale mahogany two chair-back settee, Boston, circa 1760–1780. A simple version of a very rare form. This is one of less than a dozen American Chippendale chair-back settees known to exist. The arms and square legs are adequate but simple.

Ht: 37" Wd: 72" Dp: 24½"
Dr. Warren Koontz

MASTERPIECE

Chippendale mahogany two-chair-back settee with claw and ball feet, Massachusetts, circa 1760–1780. Here rarity is combined with successful design wrought by a gifted artisan. The fine strapwork splats with shell crests provide adequate support, and blend with the finely shaped arms.

Ht: 40½" Wd: 66¼" Dp: 22½"   *Private collection*

MASTERPIECE

Hepplewhite mahogany camelback sofa with spade feet, New York, circa 1780–1790 (descended in Captain William Van Deursen family). The designation of Hepplewhite to this sofa is proper, but shows the rigidity of period assignations. The power, sweep, and virile character of this sofa epitomizes and expands the Chippendale emphasis. The dramatic curves of the crest and seat frame, the boldly flaring arms, and the outward thrust of the rear legs equal or surpass many Philadelphia Chippendale examples. The Bybees recognized the sofa's greatness and had the courage to incorporate this "transitional" sofa into their Chippendale and Queen Anne living room. Time has vindicated their foresight.

Ht: 43¾" Wd: 98¼" Dp: 35½"
Dallas Museum of Art, the Faith P. and Charles L. Bybee Collection
PHOTOGRAPH: ISRAEL SACK, INC.

Profile view.

SUPERIOR

Chippendale mahogany claw-and-ball-foot settee, Massachusetts, circa 1760–1770.** Considering the rarity of American claw-and-ball-foot settees, this camelback example would be considered a prize by most standards. If the MASTERPIECE example and its mate did not exist, this would probably be considered the ultimate expression of the form. A comparison points out that a relative rigidity of the wings and heaviness of the legs are interpreted with more finesse in the MASTERPIECE examples.

Ht: 32" Wd: 55½" Dp: 26½"
The Museum of Fine Arts, Houston,
The Bayou Bend Collection
Gift of Miss Ima Hogg

MASTERPIECE

Chippendale mahogany claw-and-ball-foot settee, Boston, circa 1760–1780.** One can only sing praises to the genius of the creator of this gem. The back has a rhythmic flow with a masterful flair to the wings. Its graceful lines combine with the beautifully formed cabriole legs to form a magnificent composition. The asymmetrical knee carving with the sculptured claw and ball feet appear on a group of related tables and chairs of Boston origin. A mate to this settee is in the Winterthur Museum.

Ht: 36½" Wd: 55½" Dp: 22½"   *Metropolitan Museum of Art*

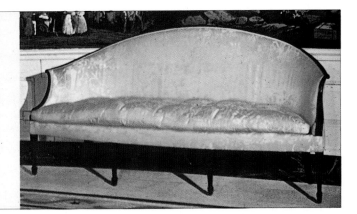

THE SWEEPING CURVE *of the back, ably controlled by the reverse curves of the arm supports, distinguishes this New York sofa in the Diplomatic Reception Room. The back legs rake; the fluted front legs rest on pointed spade feet.*

MASTERPIECE

Hepplewhite mahogany cabriole sofa with reeded legs and spade feet, New York, circa 1780–1800. This is one of the most beautiful sofas produced in New York in the Federal period. It also has the distinction of being the first gift to the renovated White House. The Diplomatic Reception Room, which is the large, oval room on the ground floor of the White House, was furnished as a gift to the nation by the National Society of Interior Designers while the Eisenhowers were in office. Israel Sack, Inc., donated this sofa, the oval back of which is most appropriate in the oval room.

Ht: 39" Wd: 81" Dp: 28"   *The White House Collection*

MASTERPIECE

Chippendale mahogany camelback sofa with peaks, molded legs, Philadelphia, circa 1760–1780. The small group of Philadelphia sofas with peaks are justly recognized as the top of the line. This example has dynamic impact due to its compact size and superb lines. The serpentine-front seat frame adds to its fluency.

Ht: 39½" Wd: 79" Dp: 30½"   *Private collection*

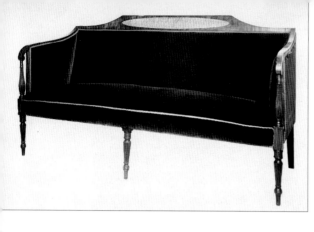

BEST

Sheraton mahogany sofa, Salem, Massachusetts, circa 1800–1810. A desirable sofa of pleasing lines. The shaped crest with oval maple panel adds to its appeal.

Whereabouts unknown

PHOTOGRAPH: ISRAEL SACK, INC.

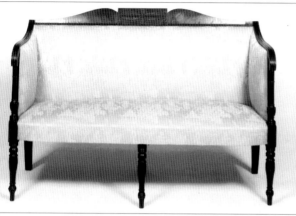

SUPERIOR

Sheraton mahogany small settee, the crest with rectangular carved center panel and shaped wings, Salem, Massachusetts, circa 1800–1815. Small American settees of this quality are extremely rare and desirable. The shape of the crest outline is typical of the design from Thomas Sheraton's *Book of Designs* and favored by Samuel McIntire.

Ht: 38" Wd: 56½"
Mr. and Mrs. Herbert Coyne

© 1983, SOTHEBY'S, INC.

MASTERPIECE

Sheraton mahogany small settee, crest carving attributed to Samuel McIntire, master carver of Salem, Massachusetts, circa 1800–1810. One of the supreme achievements of the Salem Federal school is this form of sofa with the familiar basket center, carved flowers, and drapery in a star-punch background. It is known that McIntire carved the panels for a number of these sofas, examples of which are in most major eastern museums. The discovery of this unique McIntire fully developed small settee several years ago is refreshing because it shows that many undiscovered masterpieces still can, and do, come to light every year.

Ht: 36" Wd: 55½" Dp: 24½"   *Private collection*

B E T T E R

Sheraton mahogany sofa, Salem, Massachusetts, circa 1810–1820. The grace and beauty of the SUPERIOR example is lost in this example by the heavy reeding of the legs and the boxy outline of the crest and seat frame.

Ht: 34½" Wd: 74½" Dp: 27"   *Whereabouts unknown*

S U P E R I O R

Sheraton mahogany sofa, Salem, Massachusetts, circa 1800–1810. The graceful contours formed by the bowed crest and bulbous reeded arm supports, combined with brilliantly tapered reeded legs, epitomize the Salem artisans' love of symmetry.

Ht: 36⅜" Wd: 77¼"   *Israel Sack, Inc.*

BETTER

Sheraton mahogany carved sofa, Haines-Connolly school, Philadelphia, circa 1800–1815. This sofa has carved elements that suggest the work of Philadelphia's best craftsmen, but the form lacks the finesse of the contemporary New York sofas. The carving of the crest just floats in space, rather than being contained within panels. The carved arm terminals and arm supports are relatively clumsy.

Ht: 36" Wd: 72" Dp: 27"
Whereabouts unknown

SUPERIOR

Sheraton mahogany sofa with three-panel carved crest and straight sides, made by Duncan Phyfe or a contemporary of equal rank, New York, circa 1800–1815. A considerable number of sofas of similar high quality were made for New York's prosperous patrons by Duncan Phyfe and his contemporaries. The panels are standard Phyfe motifs with ribbons and sheaves of wheat at the ends and a drapery carved center panel.

Ht: 37½" Wd: 77½" Dp: 31"   *Israel Sack, Inc.*

MASTERPIECE

Sheraton mahogany sofa with three-panel carved crest, incurvate arms, and reeded seat frame, made by Duncan Phyfe or a contemporary of equal rank, New York, circa 1800–1815. Duncan Phyfe and his competitors made sofas with incurvate arms for their more affluent customers. These sofas were of the same quality of craftsmanship and carving as the SUPERIOR straight-arm variety, but the curvilinear form exhibits greater fluidity of line. Although a number of similar sofas survive, each one of this quality can be considered a masterpiece of New York Sheraton design.

Ht: 37" Wd: 80" Dp: 32"   Private collection

GOOD

Classical mahogany sofa with incurvate legs, New York, circa 1815–1825. This is an ungainly sofa with some decent parts, particularly the nice rolled arms, but nothing seems to fit together.

Whereabouts unknown
PHOTOGRAPHIC ARCHIVES, NATIONAL GALLERY OF ART

MASTERPIECE

Classical mahogany sofa with incurvate legs, Boston, Massachusetts, circa 1810–1820. The bowed crest and seat highlighted by lunette inlay and the scrolled arm terminals add flavor to a highly successful and integrated composition.

Ht: 37" Wd: 78" Dp: 25"
Israel Sack, Inc.

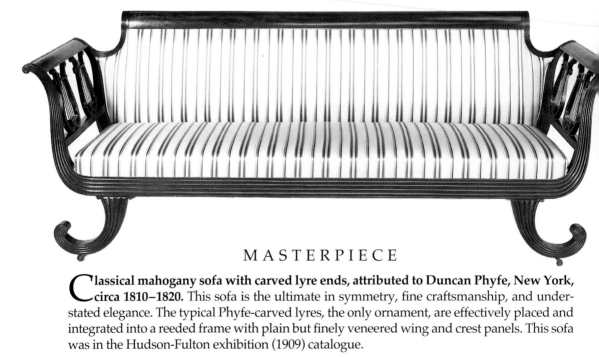

MASTERPIECE

Classical mahogany sofa with carved lyre ends, attributed to Duncan Phyfe, New York, circa 1810–1820. This sofa is the ultimate in symmetry, fine craftsmanship, and understated elegance. The typical Phyfe-carved lyres, the only ornament, are effectively placed and integrated into a reeded frame with plain but finely veneered wing and crest panels. This sofa was in the Hudson-Fulton exhibition (1909) catalogue.

Ht: 33¼" Wd: 84¼" Dp: 28"   Private collection

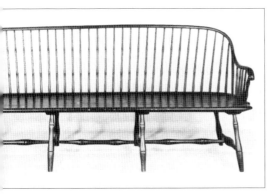

BEST

Windsor bow-back settee with roll-arm terminals, bamboo-turned legs and stretchers, Pennsylvania, circa 1800–1820. A very pleasing settee with a nice saddle seat, refined spindles, and well-formed arms. The base turnings are not as sophisticated as the following examples.

Wd: 84"   *Whereabouts unknown*

PHOTOGRAPHIC ARCHIVES, NATIONAL GALLERY OF ART

SUPERIOR

Windsor settee with serpentine crest and bulbous-turned legs and stretchers, Pennsylvania, circa 1790–1810. This Windsor maker had a great sense of proportion and design. The back is particularly satisfying where the bow arches in a serpentine outline. The leg turning is also very fine.

Wd: 76"   *Whereabouts unknown*

PHOTOGRAPHIC ARCHIVES, NATIONAL GALLERY OF ART

MASTERPIECE

Windsor settee with knuckle-arm terminals and cylinder-turned legs, Pennsylvania, circa 1770–1790. The superb modeling of the knuckle-arm terminals and the cylinder-turned legs place this settee in the highest category of Windsor artisanship. The impressive size of nine feet makes this also one of the largest Windsor settees known.

Wd: 108"   *Private collection*

TABLES

BETTER

Early maple and pine tavern table, New England, circa 1700–1730 (below). Any table of this form that can pass the test of unquestioned authenticity is desirable and rare. On this example, the turnings are relatively weak, and the legs have no rake.

Ht: 25¼" Lg: (top) 31¾"

© 1977, SOTHEBY'S, INC.

BEST

Early maple and pine tavern table, New England, circa 1700–1730 (above). The ring and bulbous turnings, though thin, are more refined than those on the previous model. The legs have a good rake, which serves to provide a more dramatic stance.

Ht: 24¼" Lg: (top) 28¾"

© 1977, SOTHEBY'S, INC.

MASTERPIECE

Early maple tavern table, retaining the original paint and surface, Rhode Island, circa 1700–1730. This gem gives a thrill to any lover of the Pilgrim era. Compact size, bold and finely modeled turnings, legs which rake in two directions, both to the front and to the side, and, most important, the miracle of the piece's condition—original paint and surfaces—make this one of the finest examples extant.

Ht: 24¼" Lg: (top) 28¾" Wd: (top) 20"
Collection of Mr. and Mrs. Israel E. Liverant

BEST

Early cherry butterfly table, New England, circa 1690–1720. Even though the ring and bulbous turnings are not as refined as those of the SUPERIOR example, the rarity of any genuine butterfly table, plus a desirable aspect, justifies a high rating.

Formerly Israel Sack, Inc.
(whereabouts unknown)

SUPERIOR

Early cherry butterfly table, New England, circa 1710–1730. This table is distinguished by its rare and desirable block and bulbous-turned stretchers as well as by more refined turnings and outstanding early aspect. The quarter round replacing the rule joint of the Pilgrim period suggests a date in the first quarter of the eighteenth century.

Ht: 27½" Lg: 37" Wd: 36½" open
Private collection

BETTER

Small maple gateleg table, Massachusetts, circa 1700–1720. Prior to the Queen Anne (cabriole leg) period, there was little variation in the form of American drop-leaf tables. This gateleg form remained fairly consistent from the last quarter of the seventeenth century (Pilgrim) to the most refined products of the William and Mary era. Their excellence (or lack of it) is expressed in the quality of the turnings and in the degree of craftsmanship, as well as their condition. The turnings on this table do not have the strength or refinement of the MASTERPIECE example.

Ht: 27" Wd: 42"   Whereabouts unknown

PHOTOGRAPHIC ARCHIVES, NATIONAL GALLERY OF ART

MASTERPIECE

William and Mary walnut gateleg dining table, Massachusetts, circa 1710–1730. This table represents the height of achievement of the form by virtue of its superb ball-and-ring turnings, its important large size, and its superlative condition. Each end contains a drawer with the original engraved brass handle secured with cotter pins. The table is branded *IS* for Israel Sack, an identification often used in the 1920s during his Boston career.

Ht: 27½" Lg: 54" Wd: 62" open   Israel Sack, Inc.

AMERICAN: MASTERPIECE

Queen Anne mahogany tray-top tea table, Boston, circa 1740–1770, from the Ladd family, Portsmouth, New Hampshire (below). This unornamented masterpiece achieves in form what its London contemporaries achieved in superb craftsmanship and ornament. The American version was formed by accomplished masters in urban centers—Boston and Newport—and can be compared more aptly with the English country version, as seen here. The apron, with its series of cyma curves and spurs, is rhythmic, and the bulged molding allows it to flow smoothly into the curve of the cabriole. Both tables have c-scrolled marginal inner borders. The cabriole leg has less knee and more of a bend than its English counterpart. The thigh thins out high, allowing for a longer, more slender ankle which breaks sharply into a crisp, waferlike platformed pad. The tray molding has a deep cove with notched corners and is integrated to the frame with a retaining molding.

Ht: 27" Lg: 28¾" Wd: 20¼"
Private collection

ENGLISH

Queen Anne mahogany tray-top tea table, domestic England, circa 1720–1750 (above). A highly desirable English tea table with a graceful apron. The shallow tray-top moldings and the shaping of the cabriole leg are typically English, with the broader knee encompassing almost half the leg and serving as a background for the carving. The leg has less bend and the foot is more understated than in a comparable American example.

© 1977, SOTHEBY'S, INC.

BETTER

Queen Anne mahogany slipper-foot tea table, Newport, Rhode Island, circa 1740–1770. The most common form of Newport tray-top tea table is the slipper-foot group. The squared cabriole leg of this table, ending in a pointed slipper foot, and the quarter-round apron molding with cyma returns are characteristic. The legs of this example have too much bulk at the knee, and they lack the finesse as well as the graceful cabriole curve which exists on the SUPERIOR and MASTERPIECE examples.

Ht: 27" Lg: 30" Wd: 20"
Whereabouts unknown

SUPERIOR

Queen Anne mahogany slipper-foot tea table, Newport, Rhode Island, circa 1740–1770. A master craftsman molded what could have been a stark, linear design into a graceful, elegant composition, using form and successful craftsmanship to achieve his end. John Goddard and the various Townsends made many such tables, but to date none has been documented. Note the graceful silhouette formed by the ridged outline of the squared cabriole leg as it flows into the pointed slipper foot.

Ht: 26" Lg: 31" Wd: 19"
Formerly Israel Sack, Inc.
(whereabouts unknown)

MASTERPIECE

Queen Anne maple slipper-foot tea table, Newport, Rhode Island, circa 1740–1770. The usual linear formation of Newport furniture is transformed into a graceful, sinuous expression more typical of Massachusetts counterparts. The cyma-shaped apron flows into a squared cabriole leg, and the boldly flaring coved tray molding integrates to the frame with a retaining molding.

Ht: 26¾" Lg: 30½" Wd: 20¼"
Private collection
PHOTOGRAPH: ISRAEL SACK, INC.

BETTER

Queen Anne maple oval-top tavern table, Rhode Island, circa 1740–1770. A better-than-average example of a popular form produced throughout New England centers and small towns. Its rural aspect is revealed in the close-cropped overhang of the top, the simple apron, and the swell of the turning (which gives the illusion of indigestion).

Ht: 29½" Lg: 30¼"

© 1978, SOTHEBY'S, INC.

SUPERIOR

Queen Anne maple oval-top tavern table, Rhode Island, circa 1740–1770. This table shows the hand of a competent cabinetmaker, although not of the stature of the Goddard-Townsend group. It is rare to find tables of this quality made of maple rather than of the mahogany or walnut more characteristic of the skilled craftsmen of Rhode Island. This example has a balanced overhang, a finely shaped apron, and a competent bulbous-turned leg.

Ht: 26¾" Lg: 36¾"

© 1978, SOTHEBY'S, INC.

SUPERIOR

Queen Anne mahogany porringer-top tea table, Newport, Rhode Island, circa 1740–1770. This form, which vies with the tray-top slipper-foot table favored by the Goddard-Townsend families, shows the careful modeling characteristic of the group. An amusing inscription under the top reads *"John Mumford was the handsomest man in New England, a gay lothario, intemperate deserted his wife, finally found dead under Arnold's Bridge just outside Providence, drowned or drunk, no one knew."*

Ht: 27¼" Lg: 33¾" Wd: 25"
Collection of Mr. and Mrs. Eddy G. Nicholson

MASTERPIECE

Queen Anne San Domingan mahogany porringer-top tea table, Goddard-Townsend school, Newport, Rhode Island, circa 1750–1770. An inspired artisan lifted the standard Newport model to exalted stature. The small scale of this table adds to the excitement of the composition. The cyma and lobed scrolling of the apron is vibrant yet professional and the finely turned tapered legs angle to balance the boldly overhanging top.

Ht: 25½" Lg: 25¼" Wd: 21"
Private collection
PHOTOGRAPH: ISRAEL SACK, INC.

GOOD

Chippendale cherry claw-and-ball-foot tray-top tea table, Middle States, circa 1750–1800. The most redeeming feature of this table is the rarity of genuine Chippendale tray-top tea tables. The legs are ineptly curved, the claw and ball feet are embryonic, and the shell carving seems applied to the knees rather than being an integral part of the leg. It is more difficult to pinpoint the center of origin of a rural table than the origin of a table in the artist-craftsman realm.

Ht: 27" Lg: 30½" Wd: 23½"
Whereabouts unknown

MASTERPIECE

Chippendale mahogany claw-and-ball-foot tea table with painted-iron tray top, attributed to Thomas Tufft, Philadelphia, circa 1760–1780. This table epitomizes the exquisite grace and beauty a master designer could achieve with a unique creation. The repeat cyma outlines of the tray borders unite with repeat outlines of the flaring retaining moldings. The sheet-iron top, with its original off-white and gilt paint, was probably the inspiration of an owner of an iron works such as Richard Edwards, who owned the Taunton Iron Works and who engaged Thomas Tufft to fashion his furniture. A comparison of this table with the Richard Edwards pier table makes this theory a plausible one.

Ht: 28" Lg: 30¼" Wd: 20¼"   **Private collection**

MASTERPIECE

Chippendale mahogany claw-and-ball-foot tray-top tea table, New York, circa 1760–1770. Less than half a dozen New York tables of this form exist. This table exudes power and, as Maxim Karolik would say, "masculinity." The cabriole legs with acanthus-carved knees and scrolled brackets terminate in typical New York sculptured claw and ball feet. The gadrooned apron borders are equally bold and skillfully carved.

Ht: 27¼" Lg: 34½" Wd: 21"
Collection of Erving and Joyce Wolf

PHOTOGRAPH: ISRAEL SACK, INC.

BETTER

Queen Anne walnut tray-top tea table, Massachusetts, circa 1740–1770. A desirable table, which does not have the refinement and grace of the SUPERIOR and MASTERPIECE. The leg is somewhat heavy at the knee, and the bulged apron lacks the tightness and complexity of the finer examples.

Ht: 26" Lg: 29¾" Wd: 19"

© 1982, SOTHEBY'S, INC.

SUPERIOR

Queen Anne mahogany tea table of diminutive scale, Boston, circa 1750–1770. The appeal of this table is aided by its small size and skilled modeling. The apron is tightly scrolled and spurred. The notched corners of the tray moldings and the crisp platformed pads add to its refinement.

Ht: 26" Lg: 26" Wd: 18"   *Private collection*

MASTERPIECE

Queen Anne mahogany tray-top tea table with candle slides, Boston, circa 1740–1770 (descended in the Brown family of Boston). At least a score of similar tables were fashioned in Boston and Newport by master artisans. They represent the height of achievement in New England tea tables and have come to be recognized as one of the major contributions of colonial design. While the Boston and Newport forms are closely allied, the strong Boston histories of most examples, as with this one, favor a Boston attribution. The candle slides add excitement to the composition.

Ht: 26¾" Lg: 29½" Wd: 18¼"
Collection of Mr. and Mrs. Eddy G. Nicholson

BETTER

Queen Anne walnut one-drawer side table, Rhode Island, circa 1740–1760. A better-than-average example of an uncommon form which suffers in comparison with its more refined counterpart. The frame is somewhat deep, with a simple apron, and there is too much overhang. The molded top edge and pad feet lack crispness and definition.

Ht: 25¾" Lg: 32½" Wd: 20¾"
Whereabouts unknown

SUPERIOR

Queen Anne mahogany one-drawer side table, Rhode Island, circa 1740–1760. The skill of this artisan is evident in the compact proportion and careful modeling of this table. The cyma-shaped brackets and pendants of the apron integrate and add finesse to the design. The crisp wafer pad feet are superior, as is the subtle tapering of the turned legs.

Ht: 26¾" Lg: 30½" Wd: 23½"
Private collection

BEST

Queen Anne maple and pine small side table, Middle States, circa 1740–1760. A pleasing little table of a scarce form. The apron outline is adequate but uninspired.

Ht: 28½" Lg: 36" Wd: 19"
© 1988, SOTHEBY'S, INC.

MASTERPIECE

Queen Anne walnut diminutive side table, Philadelphia, circa 1740–1760. This little gem would be the star in any collection. An exciting design of tightly knit cyma curves and spurs forms the apron. The beauty of the proportion and patina is matched by the skillful modeling of the drake feet and the molded top.

Ht: 29" Lg: 28" Wd: 15"   *Private collection*

MASTERPIECE

Chippendale mahogany pier table made by Thomas Tufft for Richard Edwards, Philadelphia, circa 1775. A supreme achievement. This is a symphony of grace and creative genius by one of Philadelphia's most gifted artisans. Each main element rivals the other for excellence, yet they all blend into a harmonious unit. The open fretwork is rhythmic, as is the knee carving. The gadrooned molding of the tray top has a ripply effect, like ocean waves. Truly it is an event that such an exquisite expression of Philadelphia genius is so well documented as to the owner and maker.

Ht: 33¼" Lg: 35⁷⁄₁₆" Wd: 17⅛"   *Private collection*

PHOTOGRAPH: ISRAEL SACK, INC.

BEST

Chippendale mahogany Pembroke table with spade-pierced flat stretchers, Rhode Island, circa 1770–1780. A number of tables of this form were produced in several centers, particularly Newport, New York, and Philadelphia. The shaped stretchers and pierced corner brackets add appeal to an otherwise basic table. The stretchers are beveled on the under-edge to effect refinement in spite of the thickness required.

Ht: 28" Lg: 24½" Wd: 37" open; 19" closed
Formerly Israel Sack, Inc.
(whereabouts unknown)

SUPERIOR

Chippendale mahogany Pembroke table with spade-pierced flat stretchers and serpentine-molded edge leaves with turret corners, Philadelphia, circa 1760–1780. An inspired artisan lifted the standard table into a beautiful and successful design. The stretchers are creatively formed by spade cutouts worked into a pattern of smaller and larger spades. The outer edge of the stretchers is highlighted by scrolled volutes. The serpentine top of finely figured mahogany complements the shaped stretchers.

Ht: 28¾" Lg: 31½" Wd: 22½" closed; 43" open
Private collection

BEST

Queen Anne cherry small drop-leaf table, Massachusetts, circa 1740–1760. A fine example with a nicely scrolled apron and disc-shaped pad feet. The pointed swell in the knee is a North Shore feature.

Ht: 27¼" Lg: 36½" Wd: 34¼" open
Whereabouts unknown
PHOTOGRAPH: ISRAEL SACK, INC.

SUPERIOR

Queen Anne small drop-leaf table fashioned of plum-pudding mahogany, Massachusetts, circa 1740–1760. The similarity of this table to its BEST counterpart is striking. The superiority of this table is evident in two areas: the smooth flow of the beautiful cabriole legs and the exciting plum-pudding mottled figure of the mahogany top.

Ht: 28¼" Lg: 36" Wd: 35½" open   *Private collection*

Detail of table top.

BEST

Queen Anne mahogany small drop-leaf table, North Shore, Massachusetts, circa 1740–1770. The ridged knee of the well-formed cabriole leg, indicative of North Shore centers such as Salem and Newbury-port, accentuates the curve. It combines here with a nicely scrolled apron.

Ht: 27¼″ Lg: 41½″ Wd: 40″ open
Formerly Israel Sack, Inc.
(whereabouts unknown)

MASTERPIECE

Pair of Queen Anne mahogany drop-leaf tables of rare small size, Massachusetts, circa 1740–1770. Either one of this pair qualifies as a masterpiece of slenderness and exquisite grace. The rounded knee of the cabriole leg flows into a remarkably thin ankle, which turns smoothly but sharply into a platformed pad foot. The legs, with the high-arched apron, form a dramatic outline. The square top and molded edge are in perfect balance with the base. These tables were united in what can be called a "grand reunion." As a pair, they are priceless and unique.

Ht: 25¾″ each Lg: 28½″ Wd: 28″ open   *Private collection*
PHOTOGRAPH: ISRAEL SACK, INC.

BETTER

Queen Anne cherry console table with black mottled marble top, New England, circa 1740–1770. A fairly simple version of a rare American form. The cabriole leg is reasonably competent and the retaining molding supporting the marble relieves the severity of the plain apron.

Whereabouts unknown

PHOTOGRAPHIC ARCHIVES, NATIONAL GALLERY OF ART

MASTERPIECE

Queen Anne cherry console table, gray marble top with white and yellow veins, Massachusetts, circa 1740–1770. Though all console tables retaining their original marble tops are rare, there are a score of Chippendale examples for every surviving Queen Anne console. Thus, the survival of such a graceful example is an event. The beautiful cyma-shaped apron flows into a superbly modeled cabriole leg with wafer pad foot. The overhanging marble has a quarter-round molded edge with a turret corner to integrate with the rounded corner of the retaining molding.

Ht: 27½" Lg: 54½" Wd: 26"   Private collection

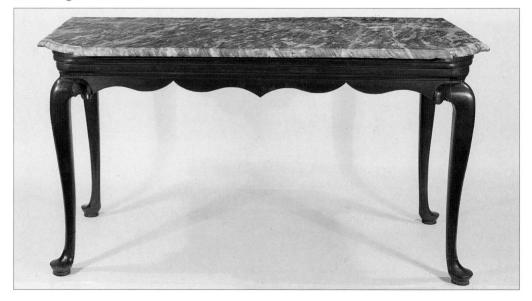

PHILADELPHIA-NEWPORT MASTERPIECES

It is hardly possible to find a better depiction of the ultimate expression of two great schools of American craftsmanship than these two console tables. Each shows masterful integration of three planes of curves in different mediums; Philadelphia is accented with well-placed carving, Newport with the use of dense mahogany that has the effect of polished marble.

MASTERPIECE

Chippendale mahogany marble-top console table, Philadelphia, circa 1760–1780. In contrast to the usual grand size of Philadelphia console tables, this table is of compact size formed from the half-round. The frame is a series of cyma and serpentine curves hewn from the solid. The horizontal plane of the frame is complemented by the vertical conformation of the apron while the center has a flowing cyma-shaped outline. The apron and frame are ornamented by shallow carving in order to accent but not dominate the undulating curves. The third plane of curves is formed by well-modeled acanthus-carved cabriole legs. The King of Prussia marble top conforms in shape and is supported by five dovetailed braces. The companion to this table is in the Pendleton Collection, Rhode Island School of Design.

Ht: 29½" Lg: 49¾" Wd: 22½"
The Museum of Fine Arts, Houston,
The Bayou Bend Collection
Gift of Miss Ima Hogg

MASTERPIECE

Chippendale mahogany marble-top console table, Goddard-Townsend, Newport, Rhode Island, circa 1760–1780. This table is a sculptured masterpiece devoid of any ornament. It accomplishes in the Newport style of stark simplicity the same mastery of the curvilinear formation that the Philadelphia counterpart does with its rococo emphasis. The cyma shaping of the frame in the horizontal plane is complemented by the apron shaping in the vertical plane. This blends with the turret corners, which are also cyma shaped. The rounding of the knees continues the line of the turrets flowing into beautifully turned ankles and sculptured claw and ball feet. The gleam of the figured, dense polished mahogany eliminates any appearance of blandness.

Ht: 26¾" Lg: 45½" Wd: 21⅞"
Rhode Island School of Design

BETTER

Queen Anne mahogany large drop-leaf dining table, Massachusetts, circa 1740–1770. This table has two things going for it: the scarcity of large Queen Anne drop-leaf tables and its descent in the Crowninshield family. The unsuccessful stiff curve of the cabriole leg, the thick ankle, and inadequate pad foot are serious design flaws.

Ht: 27½" Lg: 60" Wd: 58½" open
Whereabouts unknown

SUPERIOR

Queen Anne mahogany large drop-leaf dining table, Massachusetts, circa 1740–1770. The achievement of harmony of line and graceful flowing curves that was so natural to Massachusetts artisans is expressed here in this unadorned but beautiful dining table. The graceful cabriole legs integrate with the cyma-shaped apron by bulged, voluted knee returns.

Ht: 27½" Lg: 60" Wd: 59" open
Private collection

BEST

Chippendale mahogany claw-and-ball-foot drop-leaf table, Massachusetts, circa 1760–1780. A pleasing representative table with a nicely scrolled apron. The rounded leaves of a drop-leaf table may reduce seating capacity but soften its contours.

Ht: 27" Lg: 44" Wd: 15½" closed; 43½" open
Whereabouts unknown

SUPERIOR

Chippendale mahogany claw-and-ball-foot drop-leaf table, Massachusetts or Rhode Island, circa 1760–1780. This choice table begins where its companion leaves off. It shows exceptional craftsmanship in the modeling of the cabriole legs and the contoured voluted knee returns, as well as the fine carved detail of the claw and ball feet. The top has a balanced and well-designed overhang and the apron is finely scrolled.

Ht: 27¼" Lg: 42½"   *Collection of Eric Noah*

BETTER

Chippendale cherry Pembroke table with arched stretchers, Connecticut, circa 1770–1790 (left). A rural table with molded legs. The arched stretchers lack the finesse of the comparative tables.

Ht: 28½" Lg: 36½" Wd: 39" open
COURTESY OF CHRISTIE'S

BEST

Chippendale mahogany Pembroke table with serpentine-shaped leaves and arched stretchers, Maryland, circa 1760–1780 (right). The arched stretchers have a definitive ogival shape and blend successfully with the serpentine-shaped leaves.

Ht: 28½" Lg: 31½" Wd: 37" open
Private collection

MASTERPIECE

Chippendale mahogany Pembroke table with Marlborough feet, serpentine-shaped leaves, and arched stretchers, Philadelphia, circa 1760–1780. This superb creation ranks as one of the finest Pembroke tables fashioned in the colonies. It was illustrated in *Fine Points I* and deserves repeating in this color illustration. The fine details, such as the spiral-beaded molded legs, the gadrooned apron, and the molded edge of the top show the handiwork of a master artisan.

Ht: 28¼" Lg: 31¾" Wd: 41½" open
Metropolitan Museum of Art
PHOTOGRAPH: ISRAEL SACK, INC.

BETTER

Hepplewhite mahogany inlaid oval-top Pembroke table, Maryland, circa 1780–1800. A fine quality table, the only criticism of which is that it has a slight heaviness, particularly in comparison with the related tables shown on this page.

Formerly Israel Sack, Inc.
(whereabouts unknown)

SUPERIOR

Hepplewhite mahogany bellflower-inlaid oval-top Pembroke table, New York, circa 1780–1800. The beautiful bellflower-inlaid legs, the oval paterae, and the oval drawer panel add another dimension to this outstanding table.

Ht: 28" Lg: 32½" Wd: 39½" open; 19" closed
Formerly Israel Sack, Inc.
(whereabouts unknown)

MASTERPIECE

Hepplewhite mahogany bellflower-inlaid oval-top Pembroke table with spade feet, Baltimore, circa 1780–1800. This table represents the Baltimore school at its best. Not only are the bellflower inlay and oval paterae of the finest Baltimore tradition, but the stance, with the tapered legs flaring slightly outward, shows the mastery of a yet unidentified artisan.

Ht: 28½" Lg: 33" Wd: 41½" open; 21" closed
Israel Sack, Inc.

BETTER

Sheraton mahogany marble-top console table, New York, circa 1810–1825. A fine example of a rare form that was born perhaps ten years too late. The well-modeled but heavy reeded legs suffer in comparison with the more delicate taste of the earlier MASTERPIECE table.

Whereabouts unknown

MASTERPIECE

Sheraton mahogany marble top console table, Boston, circa 1800–1815 (one of a pair). Not only is the form extremely rare in American design, but the existence of a pair of this quality is an event. The curly maple and inlaid panel borders, as well as the inverted acanthus capitals, are features favored by John Seymour. The pierced brass galleries show a French influence.

Ht: 34" Lg: 47" Wd: 23¼"
Collection of Joy and Erving Wolf
PHOTOGRAPH: ISRAEL SACK, INC.

BEST

Classical mahogany drop-leaf library table, Duncan Phyfe school, New York, circa 1810–1835. This table exhibits the fine craftsmanship and acanthus-carved legs associated with the New York school. The concave frame adds lightness to the design. Though the bulbous column is not heavy, it is not as desirable as the acanthus-carved urn on the SUPERIOR example.

Ht: 29" Wd: 48" open
Whereabouts unknown
PHOTOGRAPH: JAMES CONZO

SUPERIOR

Classical mahogany drop-leaf library table, Duncan Phyfe or a contemporary of equal rank, New York, circa 1810–1820. The fine acanthus carving and the choice mahogany of this table is equaled by its balanced and graceful form.

Ht: 29" Lg: 46" Wd: 36" open   *Israel Sack, Inc.*

BETTER

Chippendale mahogany claw-and-ball-foot card table, Newport, Rhode Island, circa 1760–1770. This strong table employs the choice close-grained plum-pudding mahogany associated with the Newport school. Compared with the following examples, the frame is somewhat plain and the claw and ball feet are not finely sculptured and tend to sag.

Whereabouts unknown

MASTERPIECE

Chippendale mahogany claw-and-ball-foot card table, Goddard-Townsend group, Newport, Rhode Island, circa 1760–1770. An outstanding model. The use of a long drawer in the frame breaks the monotony of an otherwise plain surface. The round candle recesses, the shell and floral knee carving, and bold c-scrolls, which also accent the carved knee brackets, are effective touches.

Ht: 28½" Lg: 31¼" Dp: 15¼"
Private collection

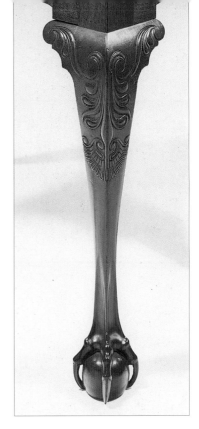

MASTERPIECE

Chippendale mahogany open-taloned claw-and-ball-foot card table, attributed to John Townsend, Newport, Rhode Island, circa 1760–1770. The magnificent open-taloned claw and ball feet, combined with the intaglio knee carving for which Newport is justly famous, are here interpreted in an equally outstanding form. The blocked center frame and conforming top add interest and strength of design, solving the problem of an otherwise plain façade.

Ht: 27½" Lg: 34½" Dp: 17"
Private collection

PHOTOGRAPH: ISRAEL SACK, INC.

BETTER

Chippendale mahogany claw-and-ball-foot five-legged card table, New York, circa 1760–1780. Compared to the serpentine form, this frame is relatively angular and severe, and the cabriole leg is somewhat stiff.

Whereabouts unknown

SUPERIOR-MASTERPIECE

Chippendale mahogany claw-and-ball-foot five-legged card table, New York, circa 1760–1780. The several varieties of New York card tables of this design represent the finest group of pre-Revolutionary New York forms. They exude powerful movement and dramatic controlled serpentine curves outlined with gadrooned or carved aprons. This table has more of a sturdy, virile character in contrast to the graceful lines of the MASTERPIECE.

Ht: 27" Lg: 33¼"   Metropolitan Museum of Art, purchased 1947, Joseph Pulitzer Bequest

MASTERPIECE

Chippendale mahogany claw-and-ball-foot five-legged card table, New York, circa 1760–1780. This table is a symphony in motion. It combines powerful currents of movement with exquisite grace, accented by the asymmetrical carved knees and gadrooned molded apron. The narrow apron and the sinuous curved cabriole legs achieve a delicacy with no sacrifice to the virility associated with the Chippendale expression.

Ht: 27½" Lg: 34" Dp: 16¼"   Formerly Israel Sack, Inc. (whereabouts unknown)

MASTERPIECE

Hepplewhite mahogany inlaid card table, labeled by John Seymour and Son, Boston, circa 1790–1810. The masterwork of the Seymour shop has few equals. This table supports John Seymour's genius and does not need the label to identify his handiwork. The bellflower drapery chains are seen in the tambour slides of the Hepplewhite desk at Winterthur and on similar examples. The satinwood panels on the tapered legs and modified spade feet also are on related Seymour pieces. This is the third labeled Seymour piece to be discovered.

Ht: 28⅝″ Lg: 36″ Dp: 18″
Collection of Mr. and Mrs. George M. Kaufman
PHOTOGRAPH: ISRAEL SACK, INC.

SUPERIOR

Hepplewhite mahogany half-round card table inlaid with American eagle and bellflower, Norfolk, Virginia, circa 1780–1800. This table bears four proud emblems of our new Republic. The eagle motifs are seen on Baltimore furniture forms, suggesting that inlaid patterns were sold by inlay specialists to more than one center. The origin of the distinctive large floral inlay has been identified as Norfolk by scholars of Southern furniture.

Ht: 30" Lg: 36" Dp: 18"   Israel Sack, Inc.

Detail of eagle inlay.

MASTERPIECE

Hepplewhite mahogany inlaid card table, bow front with ovolo ends, inlaid with American eagle in satinwood panel and urn paterae, New York, circa 1790–1810. This superb table combines a great depiction of our new national emblem with equally brilliant form. The eagle and shield on a green background serves as the central focus in a satinwood panel and is flanked by satinwood cross-banded panels in front and at the sides. Urn inlaid paterae complete the exciting design of the frame. Equally exciting are the bold incurvate ovolo ends, which serve to dramatize the central panel.

Ht: 30" Lg: 38" Dp: 18"   Private collection

BETTER

Hepplewhite cherry inlaid five-legged card table, Connecticut, circa 1780–1800. A pleasing table of high country flavor whose form and inlaid patterns do not have the finesse of the BEST and SUPERIOR examples. The frame is deeper, and the composition is more cramped.

Whereabouts unknown

SUPERIOR

Hepplewhite mahogany inlaid five-legged card table, New York, circa 1780–1800. A beautifully balanced and integrated example that does not need elaborate inlay for its excellence. The oval panels of the more slender frame serve to prevent any semblance of blandness.

Ht: 29½" Lg: 38" Dp: 18¾"
Collection of Paula Beck-Moskowitz

MASTERPIECE

Hepplewhite mahogany inlaid five-legged card table attributed to William Whitehead, New York, circa 1780–1800. The superb inlaid patterns place this table in the elite class. The delicate bellflower connected by loops is characteristic of Whitehead's documented examples. As with all great tables, the inlaid patterns are essential to the success of the design.

Ht: 29" Lg: 36" Dp: 17¾"   Private collection

BEST

Sheraton mahogany inlaid card table with figured birch or satinwood veneered frame, Portsmouth, New Hampshire, circa 1800–1815. A group of related tables with turret ends, flame-figured veneer, and checkered inlay was fashioned in Boston, North Shore centers, and Portsmouth. The reeding is not as refined as that on the MASTERPIECE.

Ht: 31" Lg: 36" Dp: 18¼"   *Israel Sack, Inc.*

MASTERPIECE

Sheraton mahogany inlaid card table with figured birch or satinwood veneered frame, Boston, circa 1800–1810. The acme of perfection of this form. The excitement of the superbly matched flame-figured veneer, enhanced by a beautiful original finish, is seen here on a table of equal competence. The bulbous, reeded tapered legs are of the highest quality.

Ht: 29½" Lg: 37" Dp: 18   *Private collection*

BETTER

Sheraton mahogany serpentine-front card table with turret ends, oval satinwood or birch panel center, Massachusetts, circa 1800–1810. The legs are the only weakness to this table. The reeding begins and ends abruptly, with multiple turnings above and below that lack the finesse of the legs of the SUPERIOR table. The top has fine figured grain but lacks a cross-banded or inlaid edge.

Ht: 30" Lg: 37"   Whereabouts unknown

PHOTOGRAPHIC ARCHIVES, NATIONAL GALLERY OF ART

SUPERIOR

Sheraton mahogany serpentine-front card table with turret ends, oval satinwood or birch panel center, Massachusetts, circa 1800–1810. In graceful form, skillful craftsmanship, and brilliant design, this table excels. The fine tapered reeding is contained in ringed terminals, ending in bulbous feet. The flame-figured oval is framed in a carefully mitered cross-banded mahogany panel, with cross-banding forming the edges of the tops and apron. The flame satinwood or birch veneer flows in uninterrupted continuity on the front, turrets, and sides.

Ht: 29½" Lg: 38½" Dp: 17½"
Israel Sack, Inc.

GOOD

Classical mahogany card table with carved lyre pedestal, New York, circa 1810–1825 (right). The acanthus-scrolled volutes have a spidery effect and interfere with the unity of the composition. The breadth of the frame seems slightly inadequate.

Ht: 29½" Lg: 34¾"
Whereabouts unknown

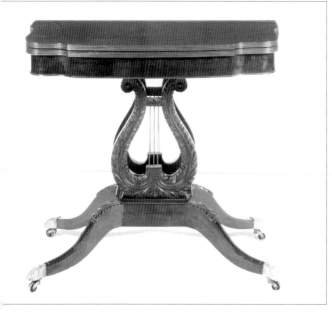

BETTER

Classical mahogany card table with carved lyre pedestal, Philadelphia, circa 1810–1825 (left). A desirable table with a more balanced composition. The finely carved lyre seems to dominate. The tightly knit carving, the abbreviated knee panel, and the frame outline are typical Philadelphia features.

Ht: 29" Lg: 33½" Dp: 16½"
© 1988, SOTHEBY'S, INC.

SUPERIOR

Classical mahogany card table with carved lyre pedestal, Duncan Phyfe or a contemporary, New York, circa 1810–1820 (right). A choice, well-integrated table. The acanthus carving of the lyre and outsplayed legs are typical of the Classical forms documented as the work of Duncan Phyfe and several of his contemporary competitors. Note the beautiful patterns of the veneered top and frame.

Ht: 29½" Lg: 36" Dp: 18"
Israel Sack, Inc.

MASTERPIECE

Classical mahogany card table with carved lyre pedestal, attributed to Michael Allison, New York, circa 1810–1820. This table rises above its contemporaries by merit of the graceful splay of the acanthus-carved legs. The leaf carving on the beautifully formed lyres is a variant from the usual and is repeated on the side edges. The attribution to Allison is based on the relationship of the drapery-carved panel to that on a documented card table by that maker.

Ht: 31¼" Lg: 36" Dp: 17½"   *Collection of Mr. and Mrs. Allen Freedman*

BETTER

S heraton mahogany serpentine-shaped card table, Massachusetts, circa 1800–1810. The carved basket of fruit was the favorite motif of Samuel McIntire and was preserved on a number of furniture masterpieces and architectural interiors in Salem. His elements were copied by other carvers, some of nearly equal ability. This carving is guaranteed not to be by McIntire. Comparison with the MASTERPIECE leaves no doubt of this fact. The form is stilted and the reeding and foot turning crude, but it suffers only in comparison with the work of the masters.

Ht: 28" Lg: 36½" Dp: 18"
Whereabouts unknown

Detail of basket.

MASTERPIECE

S heraton mahogany serpentine-shaped card table, attributed to Samuel McIntire, Salem, Massachusetts, circa 1800–1810. This table combines the craft of the master carver working with an equally competent cabinetmaker. The table would be outstanding without the carved elements by virtue of the mastery of its form, the selection of choice San Domingan mahogany, and the superb bronze patina that it has acquired. The carved basket is in deep relief. The attribution to McIntire is based as much on the precision and skill of his carved elements, equaled by few, if any, Salem carvers, as on the familiar motifs themselves.

Ht: 30" Lg: 36½" Dp: 18"   *Private collection*

Detail of basket.

BETTER

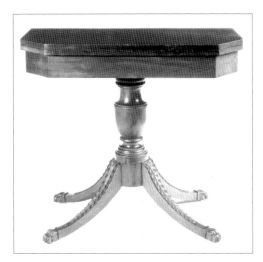

Classical mahogany card table with acanthus carving, Duncan Phyfe school, New York, circa 1815–1830. While the carving and carefully chosen veneer is of first quality, the lack of lift of the outsplayed legs and the bulk of the urn column do not match the standards of Phyfe or his top-notch competitors.

Ht: 30" Lg: 35"   *Whereabouts unknown*

PHOTOGRAPHIC ARCHIVES, NATIONAL GALLERY OF ART

Detail of base.

SUPERIOR-MASTERPIECE

Classical mahogany mechanical clover leaf–shaped card table with satinwood veneered frame, made by Duncan Phyfe or a contemporary of equal rank, New York, circa 1810–1825. An inch or two in thickness makes a world of difference in Classical New York furniture forms. The delicate urn and outsplayed legs with graceful lift are faced with leaf carving of the finest quality. The narrow frame is of equal quality and blends with the base in perfect symmetry. The side legs activate brackets to support the folding leaf by an iron mechanism.

Ht: 29¼" Lg: 35⅞" Dp: 17¾"   *Collection of Robert Rosenberg*

GOOD

Classical mahogany four-column card table, New York, circa 1815–1830. The scrolled terminals of the outsplayed legs end nowhere and disturb the unity of the base. The placement of the columns gives a cramped effect.

Ht: 30½" Lg: 37" Dp: 18"

© 1988, SOTHEBY'S, INC.

BETTER

Classical mahogany four-column card table, New York, circa 1815–1825. This table is definitely more fluent and graceful than the GOOD example, but the top does not seem adequately supported by the slender, closely placed columns

Ht: 28½" Lg: 37"

PHOTOGRAPHIC ARCHIVES, NATIONAL GALLERY OF ART

MASTERPIECE

Classical mahogany four-column card table, attributed to Duncan Phyfe, New York, circa 1805 (descended in the Hoyt family). By broadening the platform and placing the spiral and acanthus-carved columns in the corner to integrate with the acanthus-carved outsplayed legs, this table achieves perfect balance. The beauty is enhanced by a golden patina.

Ht: 30" Lg: 36" Dp: 18½"
Collection High Museum of Art, Atlanta, Georgia; purchase with funds from the Decorative Arts Endowment and funds donated by William N. Banks, Jr., to the Decorative Arts Acquisition Trust, 1992.373

BETTER

One of a pair of Empire or Classical card tables with carved eagle pedestals, New York, circa 1835–1845. This and the MASTERPIECE present an interesting contrast because the carving shown in the eagles on both tables is of comparable quality. It was therefore probably not the ability of the carver, but the demand of the client that resulted in the clumsy, grotesque legs that support our national bird.

Ht: 31½" Lg: 36½" Dp: 18"

© 1988, SOTHEBY'S, INC.

MASTERPIECE

Classical mahogany card table with carved eagle pedestal, possibly Duncan Phyfe, New York, circa 1820–1825. Here, our proud national bird is supported on gracefully out-splayed acanthus-carved legs and supports a more refined top with richly figured veneer. The lion mask fronting the plinth shows the influence of the classics. The beauty is enhanced by a golden patina.

Ht: 29½" Lg: 36" Dp: 19"   Museum of Fine Arts, Boston

GOOD

Chippendale mahogany tripod dishtop candlestand with urn column, Pennsylvania, circa 1760–1790. The satisfactory pedestal and top are spoiled by a weak and boardlike cabriole leg.

Whereabouts unknown

BETTER

Chippendale mahogany tripod dishtop candlestand with urn column, Philadelphia, circa 1770–1790. This table has a finely turned urn column, but the urn takes up too much room in proportion to the pedestal. This makes the column look bulky.

Ht: 27½" Diam: 18¾"

© 1977, SOTHEBY'S, INC.

SUPERIOR

Chippendale mahogany tripod dishtop candlestand with urn column, Philadelphia, circa 1780–1790. This stand displays the finest proportion with excellent turning and modeling of the cabriole legs. Note the rounded contour of the knee and the perfect ratio of the knee, ankle, and pad foot. The urn column is finely turned.

Ht: 28½" Diam: 20½"
Collection of Dr. Sigmund R. Sugarman

BETTER

Chippendale walnut tripod dish-top candlestand, Philadelphia, circa 1760–1780. This form is the most popular of Philadelphia candlestands with the ball-and-ring pedestal, bird-cage support, and dish top. The rating of this form depends on the finesse of the column and the stance of the cabriole legs. In this example the column is slightly thick with little taper and the legs do not have the lift seen in the SUPERIOR example.

Whereabouts unknown

SUPERIOR

Chippendale mahogany tripod dish-top candlestand, Philadelphia, circa 1760–1780. This table exhibits perfection in modeling and flawless proportions. The cabriole legs have subtly rounded knees and excellent lift to the ankles with platformed pad feet. The ball-and-ring-turned column has a slender tapering shaft and the one-piece top is in balanced ratio to the base.

Ht: 29" Diam: 22"   Private collection

MASTERPIECE

Chippendale mahogany tripod dish-top candlestand with claw and ball feet, Philadelphia, circa 1760–1780. This master craftsman elevated the traditional Philadelphia candlestand to the status of art. To begin with, claw-and-ball-foot candlestands are rare and these feet are sharply sculptured. The cabriole legs have a superb stance and are accented by restrained knee carving. The fluted shaft of the pedestal and the beaded ring of the ball turning are added touches. This gem is worth several times that of even its fine standard companions.

Private collection: Formerly collection of Mrs. Charles Hallam Keep

BEST

Chippendale cherry tripod candlestand with spurred knee outline, Connecticut Valley, circa 1780–1800 (left). This table expresses the vibrant and creative spirit of the craftsmen of this region with its dramatic leg outline, nicely turned urn column, and inlaid top.

Ht: 27" Top: 17" x 17⅜"   Private collection

SUPERIOR

Chippendale cherry tripod candlestand with spurred knee outline, Connecticut Valley, circa 1780–1800 (right). This table combines the drama of the BEST example with skillful modeling and an integration more often seen in urban centers.

Ht: 26½" Top: 16¼" x 16"
Private collection

BETTER

Chippendale curly maple tripod dish-top tea table with birdcage support, Pennsylvania, circa 1760–1780. This table has the same basic elements as the SUPERIOR example, but with a world of difference. The column is quite heavy for the slender legs, and the legs do not have the lift or the graceful curves as those of its counterpart. This form, common in mahogany or walnut, is rare in curly maple.

Ht: 27½" Diam: 31¼"

© 1977, SOTHEBY'S, INC.

SUPERIOR

Chippendale mahogany tripod dish-top tea table with birdcage support, Philadelphia, circa 1760–1780. In its unadorned form, this table has as much finesse as its more important companions with piecrust tops and claw and ball feet. The elliptical ball and ring column, with slender tapering shaft, is in perfect balance with the graceful legs.

Ht: 28½" Diam: 35"
Collection of Ida Belle Young

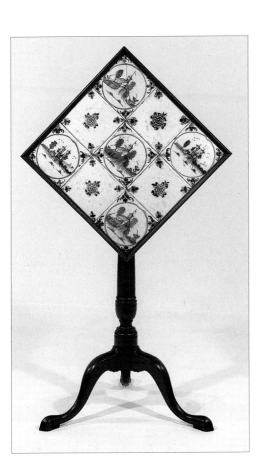

MASTERPIECE

Chippendale birch tripod candlestand, square top with imported Delft tiles, Massachusetts, circa 1760–1770. Delft tiles from England or Holland are used on a few tea tables of New England origin, but this is the first example on a candlestand. The original tiles are framed in molded dish strips. The top tilts on the diagonal effecting a diamond pattern. Fortunately, the stand itself is of high quality.

Ht: 28¼″ Diam: 16″   Private collection

PHOTOGRAPH: ISRAEL SACK, INC.

BETTER

Chippendale mahogany tripod dish-top tea table, Philadelphia, circa 1760–1780. The ball-and-ring-turned pedestal and dish top are beyond criticism. The legs have two weaknesses: the thigh and ankle are almost the same thickness and lack the contouring of the SUPERIOR example, and the claw and ball feet lack the sharply defined talons seen on finer examples.

Ht: 27³/₄" Diam: 33¹/₂"
Whereabouts unknown
PHOTOGRAPH: ISRAEL SACK, INC.

Detail of base.

SUPERIOR

Chippendale mahogany tripod dish-top tea table, Philadelphia, circa 1760–1780. The bold stance of the cabriole legs highlighted with acanthus carving and beautifully sculptured claw and ball feet surpass these elements on many piecrust tables. The lift of the ankles, the finely carved knees, the modeling of the legs, and the sculptured claw and ball feet attest to the superiority of the craftsman who fashioned this table.

Ht: 28¹/₄" Diam: 35¹/₂"   Private collection

Detail of base.

GOOD

Chippendale cherry tripod tea table with birdcage support, Connecticut, circa 1770–1790 (above). The slender column and turning are too spindly for the provincial spiral urn they support. The pad feet are heavy and attenuated, giving the large tripod a spidery look.

Whereabouts unknown
PHOTOGRAPHIC ARCHIVES, NATIONAL GALLERY OF ART

BETTER

Chippendale mahogany tripod tea table with birdcage support, Rhode Island, circa 1760–1780 (below). The spiral urn of this example is more integrated with the column, which is slightly heavy. The carved knees are a plus, but the claw and ball feet are too small.

Ht: 27¾" Diam: 31¾"

© 1978, SOTHEBY'S, INC.

SUPERIOR

Chippendale mahogany tripod dish-top table, Rhode Island, circa 1760–1780. This table, which tilts on a maple block, is far superior to, and more valuable than, the preceding examples because of its fine craftsmanship and skillful elements. The spiral urn, fluted column, and stylized knee carving indicate the hand of one of the Newport masters, as do the finely sculptured claw and ball feet. The elements blend into an integrated composition.

Ht: 27" Diam: 30"
Collection of Mr. and Mrs. Philip Holzer

GOOD

Chippendale mahogany tripod piecrust tea table, Pennsylvania, circa 1760–1780 (right). A competent piecrust top is supported by a poorly designed base. It is probably just as well that we don't see the stationary view. The cabriole legs lack tension and end in embryonic claw and ball feet.

Whereabouts unknown

BETTER

Chippendale mahogany tripod piecrust tea table, Pennsylvania, circa 1760–1780 (left). A better than average table with a few weaknesses. The legs have a somewhat awkward stance, the claw and ball feet are not finely sculptured, and the column is too thin for the weight of the top. The gadrooned base molding is a rare variation.

Whereabouts unknown
PHOTOGRAPHIC ARCHIVES, NATIONAL GALLERY OF ART

SUPERIOR

Chippendale mahogany tripod piecrust tea table, Philadelphia, circa 1760–1780 (right). The table shows the hand of a competent cabinetmaker and carver. The base has a fine stance, and the bulbous pedestal is properly turned to avoid any appearance of heaviness.

Ht: 28¼" Diam: 34"   Israel Sack, Inc.

MASTERPIECE

Chippendale mahogany tripod piecrust tea table, Philadelphia, circa 1760–1780. Not only are all three elements—the legs, the pedestal, and the top—superb in their own right, but they unite into a highly successful composition. The carving has a rhythmic flow. Notice the subtle tapering of the shaft over the finely carved elliptical ball. An almost identical table in a private collection was illustrated in the Girl Scout Loan Exhibition, catalogue #612.

Ht: 28¼" Diam: 32½"   Private collection
PHOTOGRAPH: ISRAEL SACK, INC.

Detail of base.

GOOD

Chippendale cherry tripod tea table with scalloped top, Connecticut, circa 1770–1790. A rural version of a group of Hartford-vicinity tables with similar tops. The urn column, with its spindly untapered shaft, is inept, and the table seems an assemblage of parts rather than an integrated whole.

Whereabouts unknown

SUPERIOR

Chippendale cherry tripod tea table with birdcage support and scalloped top, attributed to Eliphalet Chapin, East Windsor, Connecticut, circa 1770–1790. This table, along with a companion armchair, was part of the wedding furniture of Anna Barnard of Northampton, Massachusetts. It shows the mastery that can be achieved in a highly individualistic interpretation. The Philadelphia influence is strong in the finely modeled ball-and-ring-turned pedestal with its tapering shaft, and in its equally fine cabriole legs with sculptured claw and ball feet.

Ht: 28¼" Wd: 37"   Private collection

BEST

Hepplewhite mahogany tilt-top candle stand, Massachusetts, circa 1780–1800 (left). A typical and totally satisfying candlestand. The difference between this and the SUPERIOR model illustrates the fine line between competence and inspiration.

Ht: 28½" Top: 14¾" x 21"
Private collection

SUPERIOR

Hepplewhite mahogany tripod tilt-top candlestand, Massachusetts, circa 1780–1800 (right). That the hand of an artist carries the standard form to exquisite grace is evident in the finely grained top, the spring of the bow, and the nicely modeled urn of the column, partially visible in the photograph. Note that the inner façade of the spade is arced to continue the curve of the bow.

Ht: 30½" Top: 15¼" x 22¾"
Collection of Mr. and Mrs. James Loeb

MASTERPIECE

Hepplewhite satinwood and curly satinwood inlaid tripod tilt-top candlestand, attributed to John Seymour and Son, Boston, circa 1780–1800. The Seymours are among the very few Massachusetts craftsmen to employ satinwood as a primary wood. The satinwood rays are divided by checkered inlay, and the oval patera features a fleur-de-lis and crown. This motif appears on a tall clock with fretwork made by John Bailey, now in the Currier Gallery of Art. The curly figure of the satinwood adds to the appeal.

Ht: 29" Top: 15½" x 23¾"   Private collection

BETTER

Sheraton birch and figured birch gallery table, North Shore, Massachusetts, or New Hampshire, circa 1800–1815. A pleasing rural version of a popular and useful New England form. The drawers are the most sophisticated element, with carefully chosen crotch veneer and cross-banded mitered borders. The top lacks integration with the case. The turnings and the scalloping show country workmanship.

Whereabouts unknown

BEST

Sheraton mahogany and figured birch or satinwood gallery table, Massachusetts, circa 1800–1815. A fine example by an urban artisan whose competence shows in the integration of the top with the case, the nicely reeded columns and turned legs, and the wavy outline of the shelf tray. The figured veneer drawer fronts are banded with light and dark rosewood.

Ht: 30" Lg: 19" Wd: 19"
Formerly Israel Sack, Inc. (whereabouts unknown)

SUPERIOR-
MASTERPIECE

Sheraton mahogany and figured birch or satinwood gallery table with candle slides, probably Portsmouth, New Hampshire, circa 1800–1815. This is my pick from all its contemporaries! It is exquisitely slender without being spindly. The lively figured panels are bordered in dot-dash inlay, the two-paneled drawer front tightens the composition. Its octagon ivory escutcheon suggests Portsmouth. The candle slides are a rare feature.

Ht: 29½" Lg: 16" Wd: 16"   *Private collection*

BEST

Sheraton mahogany sewing table, labeled by Jacob Forster, Charlestown, Massachusetts, circa 1800–1815. A choice documented table which deserves no criticism except in relation to its Seymour counterpart. The side sewing slide with lock is rarely seen on pieces other than those of Seymour, but proves the fallibility of absolutes. The square case is not as appealing as the comparative table with rounded corners. The reeding is less refined. This labeled table is not as valuable as the unlabeled SUPERIOR example, further proof that form and skill rather than documentation determine value among the informed.

Ht: 27" Lg: 20" Wd: 14"   *Israel Sack, Inc.*

SUPERIOR

Sheraton mahogany sewing table, attributed to John or Thomas Seymour, Boston, circa 1800–1815. Superiority is evident in the competence of the bulbous-reeded leg, the choice selection of the wood, the careful craftsmanship, and the rounded corners that soften the contour. The relationship of this table to a documented one by Thomas Seymour (Vernon Stoneman, *John and Thomas Seymour*, Stoneman, 1959 [Special Publications] plate #151) as well as the petaled knobs favored by that shop, support the attribution.

Ht: 29¾" Lg: 21" Wd: 15¾"
Private collection
PHOTOGRAPH: ISRAEL SACK, INC.

BETTER

Sheraton mahogany work table with turret corners, Massachusetts, circa 1810–1820. This table exhibits competent craftsmanship and the selection of fine mahogany. The reeding of the legs is slightly heavy and begins and ends abruptly, lacking the finesse of the subsequent examples.

Ht: 28¾" Lg: 20½" Wd: 16½"
Whereabouts unknown

SUPERIOR

Sheraton mahogany sewing table with turret corners, Seymour school, Boston, circa 1800–1815. A finely modeled example. The reeded turrets and the finely reeded tapered legs have finesse, moving it to another class from the previous example.

Ht: 28½" Lg: 21½" Wd: 17¾"
Private collection

MASTERPIECE

Sheraton mahogany sewing table with turret ends, veneered and inlaid with various woods, attributed to John Seymour and Son, Boston, circa 1800–1815. A small group of related tables are attributed to the master craftsmen of Boston. All have the dramatic tops veneered with burl center, a blistered unidentified wood border, and inlaid patterns. The edge is lunette inlay favored by John Seymour and other Boston makers. The sewing basket on the side with lock and the twin panels of flame satinwood or birch are also characteristic of Seymour. The slender reeded legs are of the highest quality.

Ht: 30" Lg: 21¼" Wd: 17"
Collection of Eric Noah

BETTER

Sheraton maple and pine end table with painted academy decoration, Massachusetts, circa 1815–1825. Even though the decoration, with a dock scene on the top is fine, the form is ordinary, with a somewhat boxy top and heavy turned legs. Since our first criterion is successful form, this must rate only BETTER.

Ht: 27½" Lg: 22" Wd: 18"

© 1988, SOTHEBY'S, INC.

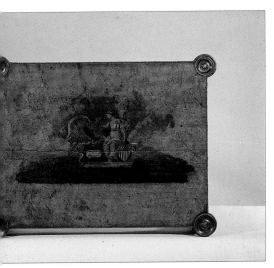

Detail of top.

MASTERPIECE

Sheraton bird's eye maple sewing table with painted decoration, Boston or Salem, Massachusetts, circa 1800–1820. Here, superb form combines with equally brilliant decoration by an accomplished artist. The finely turned legs, the reeded edge of the top and turrets, and the stance of the table are matched by the superb allegorical symbol of the new Republic that decorates the top.

Ht: 28¾" Lg: 22½" Wd: 17¼"
Collection High Museum of Art, Atlanta;
Gift of Mrs. James H. Crawford, 1977.1000.25

PHOTOGRAPH: ISRAEL SACK, INC.

BETTER

Classical mahogany work table with lyre side supports, New York, circa 1820–1830. An above average example that lacks the finesse of the finer classical models. The lyres and medial support are severely plain.

Whereabouts unknown

PHOTOGRAPHIC ARCHIVES, NATIONAL GALLERY OF ART

SUPERIOR-

MASTERPIECE

Classical mahogany work table with lyre side supports, attributed to John or Thomas Seymour, Boston, circa 1810–1820 (made for Charles Lyman, The Vale, Waltham, Massachusetts). This Boston table vies with the finest New York Classical pieces for fine design and superb craftsmanship. The graceful lyre has more animation than the more academic Phyfe versions.

Ht: 27½" Lg: 20" Wd: 14¾"
Collection of Mr. and Mrs. Stanley P. Sax

Detail: The chamfered edges of the lyre and the dark and light cross-banding show the attention paid by the Seymour craftsmen to refined detail.

BETTER

Classical mahogany tambour work table, Duncan Phyfe school, New York, circa 1810–1815. The workmanship appears to be of Phyfe quality, but the depth of the case in relationship to the base gives a top-heavy effect.

Ht: 31" Lg: 47½" Wd: 46½" extended

© 1988, SOTHEBY'S, INC.

Detail of solid grain mahogany top.

MASTERPIECE

Classical mahogany tambour work table, Duncan Phyfe or a contemporary of equal rank, New York, circa 1810–1815. Compared to the BETTER example, the balance achieved by the ratio of the tambour case with the columnar base shows the cornerstone of fine proportion to successful design. The careful modeling and the superb selection of solid and figured-grained mahogany is typical of Phyfe's exacting standards.

Ht: 30½" Lg: 20½" Wd: 13"　　*Israel Sack, Inc.*

SELECTED BIBLIOGRAPHY

(Post-1950; Organized by Date of Publication)

General American Furniture

F. Lewis Hinkley. *A Dictionary of American Furniture.* Crown Publishers, Inc., New York, 1953.

Israel Sack, Inc. *American Antiques from Israel Sack Collection,* vols. 1–10. Highland Press Publishers, Alexandria, Virginia, 1957–1991.

Helen Comstock. *American Furniture.* The Viking Press, New York, 1962.

John T. Kirk. *Early American Furniture.* Alfred A. Knopf, New York, 1970.

Dean A. Fales, Jr., and Robert Bishop. *American Painted Furniture.* E. P. Dutton and Co., New York, 1972.

Ian M. G. Quimby, ed. *Arts of the Anglo-American Community in the Seventeenth Century: The Twentieth Annual Winterthur Conference Report.* The Henry Francis du Pont Winterthur Museum and the University Press of Virginia, Charlottesville, Virginia, 1974.

Ian M. G. Quimby. *American Furniture and Its Makers, Winterthur Portfolio 13.* The Henry Francis du Pont Winterthur Museum and the University of Chicago Press, Chicago, 1979.

Jonathan Fairbanks and Elizabeth Bidwell Bates. *American Furniture 1620 to the Present.* Richard Marek Publishers, New York, 1981.

John T. Kirk. *American Furniture and the British Tradition to 1830.* Alfred A. Knopf, New York, 1982.

Harold Sack and Max Wilk. *American Treasure Hunt: The Legacy of Israel Sack.* Little, Brown and Company, Boston, 1986; Ballantine Books, New York (paperback).

Single Cabinetmaker or Group of Cabinetmakers

Ethel Hall Bjerkoe. *The Cabinetmakers of America.* Bonanza Books, New York, 1957.

Vernon C. Stoneman. *John and Thomas Seymour, Cabinetmakers in Boston, 1794–1816.* Special Publications, Boston, 1959.

Vernon C. Stoneman. *A Supplement to John and Thomas Seymour, Cabinetmakers in Boston, 1794–1816.* Special Publications, Boston, 1965.

Michael Moses and Israel Sack, Inc. *Master Craftsmen of Newport: The Townsends and Goddards.* MMI Americana Press, Tenafly, New Jersey, 1984.

Regional Forms

Ralph E. Carpenter. *The Arts and Crafts of Newport, Rhode Island, 1640–1820.* The Preservation Society of Newport County, Rhode Island, 1954.

E. Milby Burton. *Charleston Furniture, 1700–1825.* The Charleston Museum, Charleston, South Carolina, 1955.

Nicholas B. Wainwright. *Colonial Grandeur in Philadelphia: The House and Furniture of General John Cadwalader.* The Historical Society of Pennsylvania, Philadelphia, 1964.

Margaret Berwind Schiffer. *Furniture and Its Makers of Chester County, Pennsylvania.* University of Pennsylvania Press, Philadelphia, 1966.

The Colonial Society of Massachusetts. *Boston Furniture of the Eighteenth Century.* University of Virginia Press, Charlottesville, Virginia, 1974.

John J. Snyder, Jr., ed. *Philadelphia Furniture and Its Makers.* Main Street/Universe Books, New York, 1975.

Dean F. Failey. *Long Island Is My Nation: The Decorative Arts and Craftsmen, 1640–1830.* Society for the Preservation of Long Island Antiquities, Setauket, New York, 1976.

Wallace B. Gussler. *Furniture of Williamsburg and Eastern Virginia, 1710–1790.* The Virginia Museum, Richmond, Virginia, 1979.

John L. Scherer. *New York Furniture at the New York State Museum.* Highland House Publishers, Alexandria, Virginia, 1979.

John Bivens, Jr. *The Furniture of Coastal North Carolina, 1700–1820.* The Museum of Early Southern Decorative Arts, Winston-Salem, and the University of North Carolina Press, Chapel Hill, North Carolina, 1988.

Derita Coleman Williams and Nathan Harsh. *The Art and Mystery of Tennessee Furniture and Its Makers through 1850.* Tennessee Historical Society and Tennessee State Museum Foundation, Nashville, Tennessee, 1988.

Chairs: Classified by Form

Marion Day Iverson. *The American Chair, 1630–1890.* Hasting House Publishers, New York, 1957.

Thomas H. Ormsbee. *The Windsor Chair.* Deerfield Books and Heatherside Press, New York, 1962.

Robert Bishop. *Centuries and Styles of the American Chair, 1640–1970.* E. P. Dutton and Co., New York, 1972.

John T. Kirk. *American Chairs: Queen Anne and Chippendale.* Alfred A. Knopf, New York, 1972.

Patricia E. Kane. *Three Hundred Years of American Seating Furniture.* New York Graphic Society, Boston, 1976.

Robert F. Trent. *Hearts and Crowns: Folk Chairs of the Connecticut Coast.* New Haven Historical Society, New Haven, Connecticut, 1977.

Charles Santore. *The Windsor Style in America,* vols. 1 and 2. Running Press, Philadelphia, 1985 and 1987.

Benno Forman. *American Seating Furniture, 1630–1730.* A Winterthur Book, W. W. Norton & Co., New York, 1988.

Clocks: Classified by Forms

William E. Drost. *Clocks and Watches of New Jersey.* Engineering Publishers of New Jersey, Elizabeth, New Jersey, 1966.

Lester Dworetsky and Robert Dickstein. *Horology Americana.* Horology Americana, Roslyn Heights, New York, 1972.

William H. Distin and Robert Bishop. *The American Clock.* E. P. Dutton and Co., New York, 1976.

Charles S. Parsons. *New Hampshire Clocks and Clockmakers.* Adams Brown Co., Exeter, New Hampshire, 1976.

Stacy B. C. Wood, Jr., and Stephen E. Kramer III. *Clockmakers of Lancaster County and Their Clocks, 1750–1852, with a Study of Lancaster County Clock Cases by John J. Snyder, Jr.,* Van Nostrand Reinhold Co., New York, 1977.

R. H. Husher and W. W. Welch. *A Study of Simon Willard's Clocks.* Husher and Welch, Mohant, Massachusetts, 1980.

Kenneth A. Sposato. *The Dictionary of American Clocks and Watches.* Kenneth A. Sposato, White Plains, New York, 1983.

Other Furniture: Classified by Forms

Monroe H. Fabian. *The Pennsylvania-German Decorated Chest.* Main Street Press/Universe Books, New York, 1978.

Herbert F. Schiffer. *The Mirror Book.* Schiffer Publishing Ltd., Exton, Pennsylvania, 1983.

Collections

Richard H. Randall, Jr. *American Furniture in the Museum of Fine Arts, Boston.* Meriden Gravure Co., Meriden, Connecticut, 1965.

David B. Warren. *Bayou Bend: American Furniture, Paintings and Silver from the Bayou Bend Collection.* The Museum of Fine Arts, Houston, distributed by the New York Graphic Society, Boston, 1975.

Dean A. Fales, Jr. *The Furniture of Historic Deerfield.* E. P. Dutton and Co., New York, 1976.

Oswoldo Rodriguez Roque. *American Furniture at Chipstone.* The University of Wisconsin Press, Madison, Wisconsin, 1984.

J. Michael Flanigan. *American Furniture from the Kaufman Collection.* National Gallery of Art, Washington, D.C., 1986.

Christopher P. Monkhouse and Thomas S. Michie. *American Furniture in Pendleton House.* Museum of Art, Rhode Island School of Design, Providence, Rhode Island, 1986.

William Voss Elder III and Jayne E. Stokes. *American Furniture, 1780–1880, from the Collection of the Baltimore Museum of Art.* The Baltimore Museum of Art, Baltimore, Maryland, 1987.

Clement Conger and Alexander Rollins, *Treasures of State: Fine and Decorative Arts in the Diplomatic Rooms of the Department of State.* Harry N. Abrams, Inc., New York, 1991.

Charles L. Venable. *American Furniture in the Bybee Collection.* University of Texas Press, Austin, Texas, and the Dallas Museum of Art, 1989.

Elizabeth Stillinger. *The Hennage Collection.* The Colonial Williamsburg Foundation, Williamsburg, Virginia, and Highland House Publishers, Alexandria, Virginia, 1990.

Specific Concentrations Within Collections

Joseph Downs. *American Furniture: Queen Anne and Chippendale Periods in the Henry Francis du Pont Winterthur Museum.* The Macmillan Co., New York, 1952.

Charles F. Montgomery. *American Furniture: The Federal Period in the Henry Francis du Pont Winterthur Museum.* The Viking Press, New York, 1962.

Barry A. Greenlaw. *New England Furniture at Williamsburg.* The Colonial Williamsburg Foundation, distributed by the University Press of Virginia, Charlottesville, Virginia, 1974.

Berry B. Tracy. *Federal Furniture and Decorative Arts at Boscobel.* Boscobel Restoration and Harry N. Abrams, New York, 1981.

Brock Jobe and Myrna Kaye. *New England Furniture: The Colonial Era—Selections from the Society for the Preservation of New England Antiquities.* Houghton, Mifflin, Boston, 1984.

Gregory R. Weidman. *Furniture in Maryland, 1740–1940: The Collection of the Maryland Historical Society.* Maryland Historical Society, Baltimore, Maryland, 1984.

Selected Exhibitions and Exhibition Catalogues (Post-1950; Organized by Date of Exhibition)

Virginia Museum of Fine Arts, Richmond, Virginia. *Virginia Furniture, 1640–1820.* 1952.

The Essex Institute, Salem, Massachusetts. *Samuel McIntire: A Bicentennial Symposium.* 1957.

Museum of the City of New York and V. Elizabeth Miller. *Furniture by New York Cabinet Makers, 1650–1860.* 1957.

Metropolitan Museum of Art, New York. *American Art from American Collections.* 1963.

The Newark Museum, Newark, New Jersey. *Classical America: 1815–1845.* 1963.

Rhode Island Historical Society, Providence, Rhode Island. *The John Brown House Loan Exhibition of Rhode Island Furniture.* 1965.

The Detroit Institute of Arts. *American Decorative Arts from the Pilgrims to the Revolution.* 1967.

National Antique and Art Dealers Association of America. *Art Treasures Exhibition.* Parke-Bernet Galleries, New York. 1967.

Wadsworth Atheneum, Hartford, Connecticut. *Connecticut Furniture of the Seventeenth and Eighteenth Centuries.* 1967.

Baltimore Museum of Art. *Maryland Queen Anne and Chippendale Furniture of the Eighteenth Century.* 1968.

The Currier Gallery of Art, Manchester, New Hampshire. *The Dunlaps and Their Furniture.* 1970.

Metropolitan Museum of Art, New York. *19th-Century America: Furniture and Other Decorative Arts.* 1970.

Baltimore Museum of Art. *Baltimore Painted Furniture, 1800–1840.* 1972.

Western Reserve Historical Society, Cleveland, Ohio. *American Furniture in the Western Reserve*. 1972.

The New Haven Colony Historical Society and Patricia E. Kane. *Furniture of the New Haven Colony: The Seventeenth-Century Style*. 1973.

Lyman Allen Museum, New London, Connecticut. *New London County Furniture, 1640–1840*. 1974.

Museum of Fine Arts, Boston. *Paul Revere's Boston: 1735–1818*. 1975.

Baltimore Museum of Art. *Maryland Heritage: Five Baltimore Institutions Celebrate the Bicentennial*. 1976.

Philadelphia Museum of Art. *Philadelphia: Three Centuries of American Art*. 1976.

Yale University Art Gallery and the Victoria and Albert Museum. *American Art, 1750–1800: Towards Independence*. 1976.

Kennedy Galleries, Inc., and Israel Sack, Inc., New York. *The Age of Revolution and Early Republic in Fine and Decorative Arts: 1750–1824*. 1977.

North Carolina Museum of History, Raleigh, North Carolina. *North Carolina Furniture*. 1977.

The New Hampshire Historical Society, Concord, New Hampshire. *Plain and Elegant, Rich and Common: Documented New Hampshire Furniture, 1750–1850*. 1978.

Girl Scouts of the USA and Wendy Cooper. *In Praise of America: American Decorative Arts, 1650–1850*. 1980.

Yale University Art Gallery, New Haven, Connecticut, and Benjamin A. Hewitt, Patricia E. Kane, and Gerald W. R. Ward. *The Work of Many Hands: Card Tables in Federal America, 1790–1820*. 1980.

Museum of Fine Arts, Boston, Jonathan L. Fairbanks, and Robert E. Trent. *New England Begins: The Seventeenth Century*, 3 vols. 1982.

The Baltimore Museum of Art, William Voss Elder III and Lu Bartlett. *John Shaw, Cabinet-maker of Annapolis*. 1983.

The Wadsworth Atheneum, Hartford, Connecticut. *The Great River: Art and Society of the Connecticut Valley, 1635–1820*. 1985.

The Antiquarian Society of the Art Institute of Chicago, Milo Naeve, and Lynn Springer Roberts. *A Decade of Decorative Arts*. 1986.

The Cooper-Hewitt Museum, The Smithsonian National Museum of Design, New York. *Courts and Colonies: The William and Mary Style in Holland, England and America*. 1988.

Heritage Plantation of Sandwich, Sandwich, Massachusetts. *Arts of the Federal Period*. 1989.

INDEX